CAPACITY AND AUTONOMY

FOCUS ON SOCIAL WORK LAW
Series Editor: Alison Brammer

Palgrave Macmillan's Focus on Social Work Law series consists of compact, accessible guides to the principles, structures and processes of particular areas of the law as they apply to social work practice. Designed to develop students' understanding as well as refresh practitioners' knowledge, each book provides focused, digestible and navigable content in an easily portable form.

Available now

Looked After Children, Caroline Ball
Child Protection, Kim Holt
Capacity and Autonomy, Robert Johns
Making Good Decisions, Michael Preston-Shoot

Forthcoming titles

Court and Legal Skills, Penny Cooper
Adoption and Permanency, Philip Musson
Youth Justice, Jo Staines
Children in Need of Support, Joanne Westwood
Safeguarding Adults, Alison Brammer

Author of the bestselling textbook *Social Work Law*, Alison Brammer is a qualified solicitor with specialist experience working in Social Services, including child protection, adoption, mental health and community care. Alison coordinates the MA in Child Care Law and Practice and the MA in Adult Safeguarding at Keele University.

Series Standing Order

ISBN 9781137017833 paperback
(*outside North America only*)
You can receive future titles in this series as they are published by placing a standing order. Please contact your bookseller or, in the case of difficulty, write to us at the address below with your name and address, the title of the series and the ISBN quoted above.
Customer Services Department, Macmillan Distribution Ltd
Houndmills, Basingstoke, Hampshire RG21 6XS, England

CAPACITY AND AUTONOMY

ROBERT JOHNS

First published 2014 by
PALGRAVE MACMILLAN

Palgrave Macmillan in the UK is an imprint of Macmillan Publishers Limited, registered in England, company number 785998, of Houndmills, Basingstoke, Hampshire RG21 6XS.

Palgrave Macmillan in the US is a division of St Martin's Press LLC, 175 Fifth Avenue, New York, NY 10010.

Palgrave Macmillan is the global academic imprint of the above companies and has companies and representatives throughout the world.

Palgrave® and Macmillan® are registered trademarks in the United States, the United Kingdom, Europe and other countries

ISBN: 978–1–137–28645–1

This book is printed on paper suitable for recycling and made from fully managed and sustained forest sources. Logging, pulping and manufacturing processes are expected to conform to the environmental regulations of the country of origin.

A catalogue record for this book is available from the British Library.

A catalog record for this book is available from the Library of Congress.

Typeset by Cambrian Typesetters, Camberley, Surrey

Printed and bound in the UK by The Lavenham Press Ltd, Suffolk

MIX
Paper from
responsible sources
FSC
www.fsc.org
FSC® C010693

This book is dedicated to all who have experienced the frustration of losing the ability to make decisions for themselves.

CONTENTS

TABLE OF CASES

TABLE OF LEGISLATION

ACKNOWLEDGMENTS

This book is the product of several years' teaching students on qualifying and post-qualifying social work programmes, so thanks are due to all who generously shared their experience with me, and most especially to participants in Deprivation of Liberty Safeguards Best Interest Assessor courses. I would also particularly like to acknowledge the support and encouragement of colleagues at the University of East London and Tavistock and Portman NHS Foundation Trust, principally Clare Parkinson who collaborates with teaching on the Mental Capacity Act 2005.

LIST OF ABBREVIATIONS

BASW	British Association of Social Workers
BIA	Best Interests Assessor
CAFCASS	Children and Family Court Advisory and Support Service
DPP	Director of Public Prosecutions
ECHR	European Convention on Human Rights
GP	general practitioner
HCPC	Health and Care Professions Council
IMCA	Independent Mental Capacity Advocate
IMHA	Independent Mental Health Advocate
LGO	local government ombudsman
SCIE	Social Care Institute for Excellence
TCSW	The College of Social Work

USING THIS BOOK

Aim of the series

Welcome to the Focus on Social Work Law Series.

This introductory section aims to elucidate the aims and philosophy of the series; introduce some key themes that run through the series; outline the key features within each volume; and offer a brief legal skills guide to complement use of the series.

The Social Work Law Focus Series provides a distinct range of specialist resources for students and practitioners. Each volume provides an accessible and practical discussion of the law applicable to a particular area of practice. The length of each volume ensures that whilst portable and focused there is nevertheless a depth of coverage of each topic beyond that typically contained in comprehensive textbooks addressing all aspects of social work law and practice.

Each volume includes the relevant principles, structures and processes of the law (with case law integrated into the text) and highlights clearly the application of the law to practice. A key objective for each text is to identify the policy context of each area of practice and the factors that have shaped the law into its current presentation. As law is constantly developing and evolving, where known, likely future reform of the law is identified. Each book takes a critical approach, noting inconsistencies, omissions and other challenges faced by those charged with its implementation.

The significance of the Human Rights Act 1998 to social work practice is a common theme in each text and implications of the Act for practice in the particular area are identified with inclusion of relevant case law.

The series focuses on the law in England and Wales. Some references may be made to comparable aspects of law in Scotland and Northern Ireland, particularly to highlight differences in approach. With devolution in Scotland and the expanding role of the Welsh Assembly Government it will be important for practitioners in those areas and working at the borders to be familiar with any such differences.

Features

At a glance content lists

Each chapter begins with a bullet point list summarizing the key points within the topic included in that chapter. From this list the reader can see 'at a glance' how the materials are organized and what to expect in that section. The introductory chapter provides an overview of the book, outlining coverage in each chapter that enables the reader to see how the topic develops throughout the text. The boundaries of the discussion are set including, where relevant, explicit recognition of areas that are excluded from the text.

Key case analysis

One of the key aims of the series is to emphasize an integrated understanding of law, comprising legislation and case law and practice. For this reason each chapter includes at least one key case analysis feature focusing on a particularly significant case. The facts of the case are outlined in brief followed by analysis of the implications of the decision for social work practice in a short commentary. Given the significance of the selected cases, readers are encouraged to follow up references and read the case in full together with any published commentaries.

On-the-spot questions

These questions are designed to consolidate learning and prompt reflection on the material considered. These questions may be used as a basis for discussion with colleagues or fellow students and may also prompt consideration or further investigation of how the law is applied within a particular setting or authority, for example, looking at information provided to service users on a council website. Questions may also follow key cases, discussion of research findings or practice scenarios, focusing on the issues raised and application of the relevant law to practice.

Practice focus

Each volume incorporates practice-focused case scenarios to demonstrate how the law is applied to social work practice. The scenarios may be fictional or based on an actual decision.

Further reading

Each chapter closes with suggestions for further reading to develop knowledge and critical understanding. Annotated to explain the reasons for inclusion, the reader may be directed to classic influential pieces, such as enquiry reports, up-to-date research and analysis of issues discussed in the chapter, and relevant policy documents. In addition students may wish to read in full the case law included throughout the text and to follow up references integrated into discussion of each topic.

Websites

As further important sources of information, websites are also included in the text with links from the companion website. Some may be a gateway to access significant documents including government publications, others may provide accessible information for service users or present a particular perspective on an area, such as the voices of experts by experience. Given the rapid development of law and practice across the range of topics covered in the series, reference to relevant websites can be a useful way to keep pace with actual and anticipated changes

Glossary

Each text includes a subject-specific glossary of key terms for quick reference and clarification. A flashcard version of the glossary is available on the companion website.

Visual aids

As appropriate, visual aids are included where information may be presented accessibly as a table, graph or flow chart. This approach is particularly helpful for the presentation of some complex areas of law and to demonstrate structured decision-making or options available.

Companion site

The series-wide companion site www.palgrave.com/socialworklaw provides additional learning resources, including flashcard glossaries, web links, a legal skills guide, and a blog to communicate important developments and updates. The site will also host a student feedback zone.

Key sources of law

In this section an outline of the key sources of law considered throughout the series is provided. The following 'Legal skills' section includes some guidance on the easiest ways to access and understand these sources.

Legislation

The term legislation is used interchangeably with Acts of Parliament and statutes to refer to primary sources of law.

All primary legislation is produced through the parliamentary process, beginning its passage as a Bill. Bills may have their origins as an expressed policy in a government manifesto, in the work of the Law Commission, or following and responding to a significant event such as a child death or the work of a government department such as the Home Office.

Each Bill is considered by both the House of Lords and House of Commons, debated and scrutinized through various committee stages before becoming an Act on receipt of royal assent.

Legislation has a title and year, for example, the Equality Act 2010. Legislation can vary in length from an Act with just one section to others with over a hundred. Lengthy Acts are usually divided into headed 'Parts' (like chapters) containing sections, subsections and paragraphs. For example, s. 31 of the Children Act 1989 is in Part IV entitled 'Care and Supervision' and outlines the criteria for care order applications. Beyond the main body of the Act the legislation may also include 'Schedules' following the main provisions. Schedules have the same force of law as the rest of the Act but are typically used to cover detail such as a list of legislation which has been amended or revoked by the current Act or detailed matters linked to a specific provision, for instance, Schedule 2 of the Children Act 1989 details specific services (e.g. day centres) which may be provided under the duty to safeguard and promote the welfare of children in need, contained in s. 17.

Remember also that statutes often contain sections dealing with interpretation or definitions and, although often situated towards the end of the Act, these can be a useful starting point.

Legislation also includes Statutory Instruments which may be in the form of rules, regulations and orders. The term delegated legislation collectively describes this body of law as it is made under delegated authority of Parliament, usually by a minister or government department. Statutory Instruments tend to provide additional detail to the outline scheme provided by the primary legislation, the Act of Parliament. Statutory Instruments are usually cited by year and a number, for example, Local Authority Social Services (Complaints Procedure) Order SI 2006/1681.

Various documents may be issued to further assist with the implementation of legislation including guidance and codes of practice.

Guidance

Guidance documents may be described as formal or practice guidance. Formal guidance may be identified as such where it is stated to have been issued under s. 7(1) of the Local Authority Social Services Act 1970, which provides that 'local authorities shall act under the general guidance of the Secretary of State'. An example of s. 7 guidance is *Working Together to Safeguard Children* (2013, London: Department of Health). The significance of s. 7 guidance was explained by Sedley J in *R v London Borough of Islington, ex parte Rixon* [1997] ELR 66: 'Parliament in enacting s. 7(1) did not intend local authorities to whom ministerial guidance was given to be free, having considered it, to take it or leave it ... in my view parliament by s. 7(1) has required local authorities to follow the path charted by the Secretary of State's guidance, with liberty to deviate from it where the local authority judges on admissible grounds that there is good reason to do so, but without freedom to take a substantially different course.' (71)

Practice guidance does not carry s. 7 status but should nevertheless normally be followed as setting examples of what good practice might look like.

Codes of practice

Codes of practice have been issued to support the Mental Health Act 1983 and the Mental Capacity Act 2005. Again, it is a matter of good practice to follow the recommendations of the codes and these lengthy documents include detailed and illustrative scenarios to assist with interpretation and application of the legislation. There may also be a duty on specific people charged with responsibilities under the primary legislation to have regard to the code.

Guidance and codes of practice are available on relevant websites, for example, the Department of Health, as referenced in individual volumes.

Case law

Case law provides a further major source of law. In determining disputes in court the judiciary applies legislation. Where provisions within legislation are unclear or ambiguous the judiciary follows principles of statutory interpretation but at times judges are quite creative.

Some areas of law are exclusively contained in case law and described as common law. Most law of relevance to social work practice is of relatively recent origin and has its primary basis in legislation. Case law remains relevant as it links directly to such legislation and may clarify and explain provisions and terminology within the legislation. The significance of a particular decision will depend on the position of the court in a hierarchy whereby the Supreme Court is most senior and the magistrates' court is junior. Decisions of the higher courts bind the lower courts – they must be followed. This principle is known as the doctrine of precedent. Much legal debate takes place as to the precise element of a ruling which subsequently binds other decisions. This is especially the case where in the Court of Appeal or Supreme Court there are between three and five judges hearing a case, majority judgments are allowed and different judges may arrive at the same conclusion but for different reasons. Where a judge does not agree with the majority, the term dissenting judgment is applied.

It is important to understand how cases reach court. Many cases in social work law are based on challenges to the way a local authority has exercised its powers. This is an aspect of administrative law known as judicial review where the central issue for the court is not the substance of the decision taken by the authority but the way it was taken. Important considerations will be whether the authority has exceeded its powers, failed to follow established procedures or acted irrationally.

Before an individual can challenge an authority in judicial review it will usually be necessary to exhaust other remedies first, including local authority complaints procedures. If unsatisfied with the outcome of a complaint an individual has a further option which is to complain to the local government ombudsman (LGO). The LGO investigates alleged cases of maladministration and may make recommendations to local authorities including the payment of financial compensation. Ombudsman decisions may be accessed on the LGO website and make interesting reading. In cases involving social services, a common concern across children's and adults' services is unreasonable delay in carrying out assessments and providing services. See www.lgo.org.uk.

Classification of law

The above discussion related to the sources and status of laws. It is also important to note that law can serve a variety of functions and may be grouped into recognized classifications. For law relating to social work practice key classifications distinguish between law which is criminal or civil and law which is public or private.

Whilst acknowledging the importance of these classifications, it must also be appreciated that individual concerns and circumstances may not always fall so neatly into the same categories, a given scenario may engage with criminal, civil, public and private law.

- Criminal law relates to alleged behaviour which is defined by statute or common law as an offence prosecuted by the state, carrying a penalty which may include imprisonment. The offence must be proved 'beyond reasonable doubt'.
- Civil law is the term applied to all other areas of law and often focuses on disputes between individuals. A lower standard of proof, 'balance of probabilities', applies in civil cases.
- Public law is that in which society has some interest and involves a public authority, such as care proceedings.
- Private law operates between individuals, such as marriage or contract.

Legal skills guide: accessing and understanding the law

Legislation

Legislation may be accessed as printed copies published by The Stationery Office and is also available online. Some books on a particular area of law will include a copy of the Act (sometimes annotated) and this is a useful way of learning about new laws. As time goes by, however, and amendments are made to legislation it can become increasingly difficult to keep track of the up-to-date version of an Act. Revised and up-to-date versions of legislation (as well as the version originally enacted) are available on the website www.legislation.gov.uk.

Legislation may also be accessed on the Parliament website. Here, it is possible to trace the progress of current and draft Bills and a link to Hansard provides transcripts of debates on Bills as they pass through both Houses of Parliament, www.parliament.uk.

Bills and new legislation are often accompanied by 'Explanatory notes' which can give some background to the development of the new law and offer useful explanations of each provision.

Case law

Important cases are reported in law reports available in traditional bound volumes (according to court, specialist area or general weekly reports) or online. Case referencing is known as citation and follows particular conventions according to whether a hard copy law report or online version is sought.

Citation of cases in law reports begins with the names of the parties, followed by the year and volume number of the law report, followed by an abbreviation of the law report title, then the page number. For example: *Lawrence v Pembrokeshire CC* [2007] 2 FLR 705. The case is reported in volume 2 of the 2007 Family Law Report at page 705.

Online citation, sometimes referred to as neutral citation because it is not linked to a particular law report, also starts with the names of the parties, followed by the year in which the case was decided, followed by an abbreviation of the court in which the case was heard, followed by a number representing the place in the order of cases decided by that court. For example: *R (Macdonald) v Royal Borough of Kensington and Chelsea* [2011] UKSC 33. Neutral citation of this case shows that it was a 2011 decision of the Supreme Court.

University libraries tend to have subscriptions to particular legal databases, such as 'Westlaw', which can be accessed by those enrolled as students, often via direct links from the university library webpage. Westlaw and LexisNexis are especially useful as sources of case law, statutes and other legal materials. Libraries usually have their own guides to these sources, again often published on their websites. For most cases there is a short summary or analysis as well as the full transcript.

As not everyone using the series will be enrolled at a university, the following website can be accessed without any subscription: BAILII (British and Irish Legal Information Institute) www.bailii.org. This site includes judgments from the full range of UK court services including the Supreme Court, Court of Appeal and High Court but also features a wide range of tribunal decisions. Judgments for Scotland, Northern Ireland and the Republic of Ireland are also available as are judgments of the European Court of Human Rights.

Whether accessed via a law report or online, the presentation of cases follows a template. The report begins with the names of the parties, the court which heard the cases, names(s) of the judges(s) and dates of the hearing. This is followed by a summary of key legal issues involved in the case (often in italics) known as catchwords, then the headnote, which is a paragraph or so stating the key facts of the case and the nature of the claim or dispute or the criminal charge. 'HELD' indicates the ruling of the court. This is followed by a list of cases that were referred to in legal argument during the hearing, a summary of the journey of the case through appeal processes, names of the advocates and then the start of the full judgment(s) given by the judge(s). The judgment usually recounts the circumstances of the case, findings of fact and findings on the law and reasons for the decision.

If stuck on citations the Cardiff Index to Legal Abbreviations is a useful resource at www.legalabbrevs.cardiff.ac.uk.

There are numerous specific guides to legal research providing more detailed examination of legal materials but the best advice on developing legal skills is to start exploring the above and to read some case law – it's surprisingly addictive!

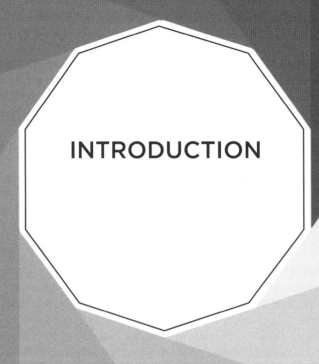

INTRODUCTION

AT A GLANCE THIS CHAPTER COVERS:

- an outline of what is in this book
- an explanation of what capacity means as a legal term
- an overview of the relevant legislation and the role of the courts in interpreting it
- an explanation of how the law is put into practice and the guidance offered to practitioners

Why social workers need to know about capacity

It may seem strange to find a book on '**capacity** and **autonomy**' in a series of books on social work law, but the practice issues surrounding the legal concept of capacity are of fundamental importance to social work. Social work is profoundly committed to principles of **empowerment**: speaking for the vulnerable, acting for the vulnerable, promoting the interests of the vulnerable, and essentially this means promoting people's autonomy. Social work is committed to maximizing people's independence, here meaning people's ability to make decisions for themselves, yet there are vulnerable people who may be at risk of abuse or injury if they exercise complete independence – so the question arises, where is it ever appropriate for that autonomy to be curtailed?

In this context 'vulnerable' covers all age sectors. Part of this book is about capacity in relation to children and young people: what children and young people can do for themselves, what happens when they are unable to make decisions for themselves, how they might be empowered through **advocacy** or, occasionally, by decisions being taken on their behalf. At greater length the book covers issues relating to capacity and empowerment for vulnerable adults – the greater length is necessary because this area of law is more complex and gives rise to a number of fundamental issues about people's autonomy. Naturally, there are particular issues for people with learning disabilities, enduring mental health problems, some kinds of physical disabilities (for example, brain injuries) and for people who lose the ability to make decisions for themselves due to the ageing process.

Readers may well be able to think of examples from experience (as a social worker, as a student on placement, or personal) where people have been placed in situations where they are potentially at risk of harm because they have made certain decisions, or failed to make certain decisions.

In each of the following chapters there will be examples of scenarios like these. It is the needs of those people that this book is intended to serve by offering knowledge of the law to those who are appointed to help them and promote their interests. Social workers working with children and families will almost inevitably find themselves having to make important decisions on behalf of children. In some cases decisions are made with which the parents profoundly disagree, and occasionally these raise substantive human rights issues: for example, where a child is removed at birth, or where arrangements are made for adoption. A social worker working with young people may have encountered a person with anorexia whose life is in serious danger, yet the young person persistently refuses to eat or give consent to medical treatment. Parents may be beside themselves with understandable anxiety and desperate to know what can be done: a legal question just as much as it is an ethical and social work practice question. A social worker working with people with learning disabilities may decide that it is best for a young adult to be placed away from home for a trial period, but what if the parent objects? A mental health social worker may have arranged for the discharge of someone from hospital into a residential home – necessary as the service user would not be able to manage independently in the community – yet whilst in the home the service user reverts to excessive use of alcohol that drives them to threaten other residents to the extent that staff demand to know what can be done to 'control' this behaviour and set boundaries. A social worker working with older people will invariably come across cases where someone appears to have lost the ability to look after their own financial affairs. Yet what can be done if the older person themselves does not realize this, and refuses to let anyone else help them, despite the all too obvious evidence of potential financial abuse?

These are typical of the kinds of scenarios which will be covered in this book. All of them have some common features.

The first commonality is that they all involve issues to do with people's ability to make decisions for themselves. The second common feature is the suggestion in each case that someone's autonomy should be overridden and that there may be perfectly justifiable reasons for doing this. The third feature is that the law has something to say in each case – the law allows for decisions to be made for other people in cases like these, at least to some extent. The key question, however, is to what extent and when? The fourth feature relevant to social work practitioners is that it is not obvious how to proceed, for in each case there is a dilemma. Social work as a profession is committed to promoting autonomy through empowerment by encouraging people to make decisions for themselves. Yet there is a duty to safeguard people, and sometimes protection can only be offered by declaring that people do not have the ability to make decisions for themselves in some important areas of their lives. So each of the examples represents the kinds of challenges which social workers have to face.

Which law is relevant to the challenges these cases pose? That is precisely what this book addresses. It is unlikely that social workers will be familiar with all aspects of the relevant legislation – after all, that is what this book is about – although hopefully some of it may have been covered to some extent in basic introductory courses in social work law. This book assumes some basic knowledge of social work law principles and practice. Key pointers as to what readers need to know are indicated in the editor's 'Legal skills guide' at the start of this book. Specifically, for this book it is important to be clear about:

- the differences between **statute law** and **common law**;
- the functions of different kinds of courts (although further explanations will be offered in this book, particularly in relation to the **Court of Protection**);
- the status of Acts of Parliament, regulations, **Codes of Practice**, ministerial guidance, National Frameworks and local authority policy.

If readers are at all uncertain about any of these, as well as looking at the 'Legal skills guide', it might be worth revisiting the relevant sections of some basic social work law textbooks (Johns, 2011; Brammer, 2013; Brayne and Carr, 2013).

The particular scenarios are either actual cases or based on real-life cases. If the scenarios pose familiar dilemmas, or if there is doubt about how to deal with these kinds of problems, then this book is well chosen. Subsequent chapters set out how the law addresses these issues, adopting a case study approach which includes discussion of key legal cases. The kinds of examples of challenges to practice highlighted above are addressed in each of the following chapters, which offer the information needed to ensure that practitioners know about the legislation that is relevant to them.

The law covered in this book relates to England and Wales. Many of the general principles would also apply in Scotland and Northern Ireland but some of the key legislation, for example, the Mental Capacity Act 2005, does not apply in those countries and the law of Scotland in particular is fundamentally different in some respects.

What is in this book

This chapter begins by presenting an overview of what is meant by the legal term 'capacity'. For the kind of people social workers deal with on an everyday basis, capacity is an important issue since it sets some boundaries about people's ability to make decisions for themselves. In some cases, the implications of assuming that people can make decisions themselves may be harmful, as in the case of someone who in 'manic' phases spends far more money than they have but finds it difficult to argue that they are not responsible for the inevitable ensuing debts. By contrast, outsiders find it difficult to understand how older people who, in their eyes, are clearly at risk of self-neglect are allowed, indeed encouraged, to remain in their own homes on the grounds that that is what they want to do. So it really is essential that social workers and healthcare professionals know about these boundaries.

In this chapter therefore are set out some legal principles in relation to personal accountability and capacity. Here an important distinction is made between the law relating to adults and children, since generally the law assumes that adults are capable of making decisions for themselves, whereas there is a very broad principle that children have decisions made for them.

This is followed by a general overview of legislation relevant to these areas. Here the importance is underlined, in terms of legal decision-making, of the role of the courts in common law, using ancient principles that allow the courts to make decisions for people who, for whatever reason, do not appear to be able to make decisions for themselves.

Finally, in relating all of this to everyday practice, the chapter highlights the importance of the various Codes of Practice and the core principles enshrined in the various pieces of legislation. As always, the law does not tell social workers what to do, law can never be used as a determinant of sound professional practice. Good practice has to be based on the application of skills and knowledge within the framework that is created by law and policy.

This book aims to set out the legal framework in relation to a crucial area of social work practice – empowerment of some of the most vulnerable members of society. So the remainder of this book covers the key areas of social work practice in relation to capacity and empowering people by encouraging them to be as autonomous as possible.

Chapter 1 examines particular issues that arise regarding children and young people and decision-making. What are the limits to their autonomy? What can young people decide for themselves regarding consent to medical treatment, for example? How does the law relating to capacity of minors connect to the Mental Capacity Act 2005, **care proceedings** and other forms of legal intervention? Chapter 1 includes an overview of judicial decisions in this area.

Chapter 2 traces the development of the key area of the law that governs capacity in relation to adults, namely the Mental Capacity Act 2005. In addition, all law has to be connected to human rights legislation so it is important to be able to interpret the law and engage in practice that is compliant with the **European Convention on Human Rights** (ECHR). This becomes particularly contentious when it applies to decisions for children of parents with learning disabilities, to whom there are dual obligations under the Mental Capacity Act 2005 and the Children Act 1989 in the Convention context.

Chapter 3 explores the practice side of the Mental Capacity Act 2005 in more detail. It outlines the principles made explicit in the Act and introduces a number of examples where these principles apply. The chapter also focuses on what is meant by capacity, and what – from a legal standpoint – needs to be assessed. This will include consideration of people's general rights to make certain decisions and arrangements in anticipation of losing capacity at some stage in their lives through, for example, making **advance decisions**.

Chapter 4 examines the intersection of the law in relation to capacity with the law relating to mental health. Here one concern is the extent to which people with serious mental health problems can be held accountable for their actions. Another issue for practitioners is deciding whether mental health or mental capacity legislation should be used in a particular case, and to what extent people with problematic mental health retain the capacity to make decisions for themselves – about treatment for a physical condition, for example.

Chapter 5 begins by offering an overview of the social work law, for both children and adults, that addresses deprivation of liberty. It then focuses specifically on the **Deprivation of Liberty Safeguards** introduced by the Mental Health Act 2007 to permit direct control over the lives of people who fall outside the remit of mental health legislation, but have clearly lost the ability to manage their own lives, or at least make decisions in relation to one particular area of their lives. There have been a number of important related case law decisions of which practitioners need to be aware.

Chapter 6 looks at the more general issue of advocacy and safeguarding – in the sense of looking after people's interests. For children involved in legal proceedings, this centres on the role of the children's **Guardian**. For adults, there are a number of avenues for empowerment. So in this chapter reference will be made to the various legal mechanisms available to people who do not have the capacity to manage their own affairs, for example, **Lasting Power of Attorney**. Included here also is coverage of the roles of people and agencies who have specific responsibilities: the **Children and Family Court Advisory and Support Service** (CAFCASS), the Court of Protection, the **Public Guardian**, and **Independent Mental Capacity Advocates** (IMCAs), for example.

In each of Chapters 1 to 6 reference will be made to relevant legislation with a demonstration of how it has been employed in real cases or might apply in some fictitious, yet realistic, case scenarios. Wherever appropriate, reference will also be made to relevant case law which will be highlighted separately from the main text.

Capacity as a legal term

Ability, competence, facility, faculty, and power are all terms suggested by a thesaurus as alternatives to the word capacity. Yet they are not quite synonyms. The legal term capacity does not just refer to the physical or mental ability to make decisions. Nor does it imply any level of skill or competence in making decisions. Part I of the Mental Capacity Act 2005 makes it clear that capacity refers to the legal power and ability to make any kind of decision, including unwise decisions (s. 1(4) Mental Capacity Act 2005). Indeed the meaning of capacity in law texts has a more precise meaning than the word capacity in its general everyday sense. Capacity in law refers to accountability – the extent to which an individual is responsible for, and can be obliged to answer for, their actions – and decision-making rights, that is, the power to enter into legal relations, such as getting married or signing a contract to buy a house. As a prerequisite for being able to do the latter an individual is assumed to have a 'sound mind' and perception of the nature and consequences of their actions.

What if they do not have this kind of 'sound mind'? As far as accountability is concerned, readers will already be familiar with cases in criminal law where it is successfully argued that someone with serious mental health difficulties is not fully accountable for their actions. This does not ignore their actions but substitutes detention in hospital for punishment such as a custodial sentence (imprisonment would assume that people knew what they were doing at the time of committing an offence and knew that it was wrong). This detention in a psychiatric hospital is justified on the grounds that their lack of awareness of their actions is related to an underlying serious '**mental disorder**'. Much of the law relating to this can be found in Part III of the Mental Health Act 1983. In civil law, which is what mainly concerns social workers in practice and is the principal focus of this book, a number of pieces of legislation are relevant. These will be outlined in the next section, but as a prelude to this, it is important to recognize that there are some generally accepted legal principles that apply here. Some of these may seem obvious but are nevertheless worth reiterating as their application can have unintended consequences.

The first key principle is that the law assumes that all adults are fully accountable for their actions and have absolute rights to make whatever lawful decision they wish – lawful meaning not proscribed or disallowed. So an adult might be persuaded to spend all the money they have (and more if they have a credit card) on a lavish cruise around the world but, if they could not really afford it, they are then responsible for the ensuing bankruptcy! They cannot then go into a shop, buy a gun, and shoot the person who cunningly persuaded them to blow their money on the trip: firstly because the law will not allow them to buy a gun without a licence, and secondly the law unsurprisingly does not allow them to harm others, and sets out a range of penalties if they do. More problematic is the situation alluded to earlier where someone has psychotic episodes during which they spend too much money; the contracts entered into with the various traders and credit companies do not automatically or necessarily become invalid on mental health grounds. Potentially the contracts could be enforceable. There is no presumption that temporary lack of awareness somehow invalidates the legal status of agreements 'freely' entered into.

The second assumption is the reverse of the principle that applies to adults. Children are not fully accountable for their actions and cannot make decisions for themselves until such time as the law allows them to do so. Readers will be familiar with the fact that in criminal law offences by children and young people are dealt with quite separately and differently by the courts. No child under the **age of criminal responsibility** (age ten in England and Wales) can be held accountable for their actions. The range of measures courts can use to sanction the behaviour of ten to 17-year-olds are applied according to age and court interpretation of the extent to which the young person understood the nature of their action and is to be held accountable for it (most of this law is now to be found in the Criminal Justice and Immigration Act 2008; see also further reading at the end of this chapter). As regards decision-making, courts have been much exercised with the issue of who decides in cases where young people need or ask for medical treatment. The fundamental principle is that parents decide for children unless the law says otherwise. The law does now say otherwise in relation to 16 and 17-year olds, and also has decreed otherwise in a number of case law decisions which will be explored in chapter 3.

On-the-spot questions	1 What is the difference between the legal term 'capacity' and what capacity might mean in general everyday conversation? 2 What are the implications of the assumption that adults are fully accountable for their actions? 3 Where might this assumption have serious consequences for an individual?

For the answer to the first question look back at the discussion at the start of this section concerning capacity as a legal term; see also chapter 4 of the *Mental Capacity Act 2005 Code of Practice* (Department for Constitutional Affairs, 2007) Assumptions that adults are fully accountable can have all sorts of implications with different degrees of consequences. There can be serious consequences in cases where, for instance, an adult allows themselves to be persuaded by an unscrupulous relative to part with treasured possessions, where they are encouraged to foster or engage in relationships which could be harmful to them, or where they incur large debts for something they do not really need without thinking through the consequences. These potential issues relate to different service groups: older people, people with learning disabilities and – as will be discussed in Chapter 6 – mental health.

Overview of legislation and the role of the courts

This book does not cover the criminal law in relation to offences committed by people who have limited capacity and accountability for their actions. This is a whole specialist area of law which does not usually concern social workers in England and Wales in their day-to-day practice.

It is important to emphasize that the Mental Capacity Act 2005 starts from a 'presumption of capacity', meaning that it is assumed that people are entirely autonomous unless it can be demonstrated otherwise, i.e.

that they lack capacity to some extent. The Mental Capacity Act 2005 then goes on to state that a person lacks capacity if they are unable to make a decision because of 'an impairment of, or a disturbance in the functioning of, the mind or brain' and 'it does not matter whether the impairment or disturbance is permanent or temporary' (s. 2 Mental Capacity Act 2005).

Issues of capacity in health and social care therefore arise principally in relation to five groups of people:

- children and young people up to age 18;
- people of all ages with learning disabilities;
- people with a 'mental disorder' (as defined in s. 1 Mental Health Act 1983);
- people with 'functioning impairments' (for example, brain injuries, dementia);
- people with life-threatening conditions when they become unable to communicate.

In relation to the last group, this would include the rights of people to make decisions for themselves concerning possible future treatment, and occasionally decisions made by courts to discontinue treatment.

It may be worth noting in passing that this list does not include older people as such. Contrary to what some younger relatives sometimes appear to think, older people do not always lose capacity as they grow older and certainly do not automatically lose their rights to self-determination and decision-making when they get to a certain age. This point is now explicitly acknowledged in legislation: 'a lack of capacity cannot be established merely by reference to a person's age or appearance' (s. 2(3)(a) Mental Capacity Act 2005). Of course, it is true that as people grow older they are more vulnerable to certain kinds of medical conditions which may affect their capacity, dementia being an obvious example. Yet the point cannot be underlined enough: assumptions must not be made on the grounds of who people are, but assessments must be firmly based on what people can or cannot do with very clear guidance on this in Part I of the Mental Capacity Act 2005 reiterated in the *Mental Capacity Act 2005 Code of Practice*:

4.4 an assessment of a person's capacity must be based on their ability to make a specific decision at the time it needs to be made, and not their ability to make decisions in general …

4.7 An assessment that a person lacks capacity to make a decision must never be based simply on: their age, their appearance, assumptions about their condition, or any aspect of their behaviour.

4.8 The Act deliberately uses the word 'appearance', because it covers all aspects of the way people look. So for example, it includes the physical characteristics of certain conditions (for example, scars, features linked to Down's syndrome or muscle spasms caused by cerebral palsy) as well as aspects of appearance like skin colour, tattoos and body piercings, or the way people dress (including religious dress).

4.9 The word 'condition' is also wide-ranging. It includes physical disabilities, learning difficulties and disabilities, illness related to age, and temporary conditions (for example, drunkenness or unconsciousness). Aspects of behaviour might include extrovert (for example, shouting or gesticulating) and withdrawn behaviour (for example, talking to yourself or avoiding eye contact).

Department for Constitutional Affairs, 2007:42–43

Chapter 3 explores how this applies in practice and considers the extent to which the courts are prepared to allow people to make decisions for themselves, a contentious issue when people make a firm declaration that they wish to refuse certain forms of medical treatment whatever the consequences, a principle established and reiterated in a number of case law decisions.

The Mental Capacity Act 2005 was a long overdue piece of legislation. Lawyers, doctors and social workers have long recognized that the previous hotch-potch of legislation relating to people who have lost capacity was in need of reform, a point to which the discussion returns in Chapter 2. As will be explained in that chapter, a number of cases in the 1980s and 1990s highlighted the need for clarification of the law. They also demonstrated a lack of appropriate venues or mechanisms for dealing with such cases, and as a consequence the High Court was obliged to deal with cases under what is called its '**inherent jurisdiction**'. Here interpretation is needed to be made of common law, with reference to a body of case law but ultimately derived from a very ancient exercise of royal prerogative powers known as *parens patriae* under which the Crown acquired a responsibility to look after the interests of people who lacked capacity.

The High Court continues to have a role in relation to this, making decisions in certain kinds of cases including, in particular, those that involve end-of-life decisions. The Mental Capacity Act 2005 redefined and extended the role of the Court of Protection, which is now the decision-making forum for the majority of contentious cases concerning adults who have lost capacity. Allied to the court is the role of the Public Guardian who has administrative responsibilities for such matters as registering Lasting Powers of Attorney and is in effect the gateway to the Court of Protection (all of this is explained further in chapter 6). The Office of the Public Guardian is accountable to the Lord Chancellor and the Ministry of Justice. In this area of work there is no role for magistrates' courts. Appeals against High Court and Court of Appeal decisions can be made to the Court of Appeal Civil Division and, on points of law, to the Supreme Court. If human rights issues are involved a final appeal can be made to the European Court of Human Rights.

As regards relevant statutes, it is important to distinguish those that apply to children and young people, principally the Children Act 1989 with which social workers will already be familiar, and those that apply to adults. The civil law aspects of the Mental Capacity Act 2005 apply to everyone aged 16 and above, whilst legislation and case decisions regarding children and young people apply to those up to the age of 18. There is thus potentially an overlap of jurisdictions for 16 and 17-year-olds, but this is largely avoided by a restriction in the application of the Mental Capacity Act 2005 Deprivation of Liberty Safeguards to age 18 or above (Schedule A1(13) Mental Capacity Act 2005). In general terms the Mental Capacity Act 2005 is the principal Act that concerns those vulnerable adults who have lost capacity. Nevertheless adult care social workers should not lose sight of the obligations of local authorities to assess people for potential provision of community care services (s. 47 National Health Service and Community Care Act 1990) and the arrangement of such services under various pieces of legislation (sometimes with associated central government directives) such as the National Assistance Act 1948, the Health Services and Public Health Act 1968 and the Chronically Sick and Disabled Persons Act 1970.

Common law has an important role to play in this area since many case law decisions concern the application of principles handed down through the ages rather than stated explicitly in statute. This has given rise to a number of important cases that have set the context for decision-making in relation to particular groups. In relation to young people, as will be seen in Chapter 2, the *Gillick* case concerns the extent to which they can make decisions for themselves without reference to a parent

(*Gillick v West Norfolk and Wisbech Area Health Authority* [1986]). In the development of the law relating to vulnerable adults the European Court decision in the *Bournewood* case (*HL v UK* [2004]), covered in Chapter 2, has had an enormous impact.

Putting the law into practice

This book assumes a basic awareness of the role of case law in interpreting the law but it may help to clarify a couple of points. First, students often ask if case law is binding. Certainly, decisions of higher courts are binding on lower courts, but as regards courts and judges of equal status then case law is highly influential but not absolutely binding. Second, students sometimes ask how very similar cases can have different outcomes. The answer to this is simply that every single case is decided on its own merits and, even though it may look almost identical to a previous decided case, there will certainly be some aspects of difference and it is only the reason for the decision in the preceding case that is binding. For more information on understanding and accessing case law and judicial review see Brammer (2013:43–45).

In order to put the law into practice, some kind of clarification, guidance or direction is required. Quite often this will come after the main legislation itself in the form of Schedules attached to Acts themselves, or else through separate associated rules or regulations, made by ministers through Statutory Instruments. It is assumed that readers are generally familiar with the differences, so what follows are specific examples related to the law covered in this book.

Schedules are part of the Act of Parliament, usually at the end, often quite detailed, but as valid as the various sections in the main body of the Act itself. The Mental Capacity Act 2005 has seven Schedules originally part of the Act when it was passed, and two more subsequently added (confusingly Schedules A1 and 1A) so as to incorporate the Deprivation of Liberty Safeguards rules (inserted by s. 50 Mental Health Act 2007).

The process of issuing rules and regulations separately from the principal Act is convenient in that it avoids the full parliamentary scrutiny that would apply to the passage of a Bill before it becomes an Act of Parliament, but obviously such Statutory Instruments cannot change the meaning of the originating Act of Parliament, they simply clarify how it is to be implemented. In the context of capacity and adults, one example would be the Court of Protection Rules 2007. Such rules and regulations have the full force of law and are as valid as the Act of Parliament to which they relate.

Of considerable significance for practitioners are the various Codes of Practice, which provide quite detailed guidance as to how an Act of Parliament is to be implemented. Codes of Practice differ from Statutory Instruments in that they are guides, not instructions. A Code of Practice does not have the full force of law, although abiding by such guidance is strongly recommended and offers a pretty robust defence if practice is criticized. In relation to the practice areas covered in the second half of this book, the *Mental Capacity Act 2005 Code of Practice* (Department for Constitutional Affairs, 2007) is of major importance, as is the Mental Capacity Act 2005 *Deprivation of Liberty Safeguards Code of Practice* (Ministry of Justice, 2008).

All sound social work practice is firmly underpinned by notions of respect for individuals and empowerment. A commitment to the core social work principle of empowerment must surely encourage practitioners to consider ways in which the law can be used to promote people's rights, encourage people to participate in decision-making, and generally enhance the quality of people's lives through promoting autonomy. Empowerment is a key concept in social work law and ethics, incorporating social justice principles and values (Dalrymple and Burke, 2006; Banks 2012: especially 152–54). Empowerment lies at the heart of social work practice. It is included in the Health and Care Professions Council (HCPC) *Standards of Proficiency for Social Workers in England* which includes 'concepts of participation, advocacy and empowerment' that social workers must 'understand in relation to social work practice' (HCPC, 2012: para. 13.4). The British Association of Social Workers (BASW) *BASW Code of Ethics* Principle 7 states a number of ways social work is about 'empowering people' and elsewhere (2.3 and 2.5) the Code encourages social workers to enable people to be included 'in all aspects of decisions and actions affecting their lives' and 'focus on the strengths of all individuals' (BASW, 2012).

There are a number of ways in which legislation covered in this book helps to promote empowerment. The adoption of the Fraser principles (set out in judgment in *Gillick v West Norfolk and Wisbech Area Health Authority* [1986]) as guidelines for professionals discerning whether young people can make important decisions themselves has undoubtedly moved practice away from the notion that only parents are able to make decisions for under-16s.

For vulnerable adults it is enormously helpful to have good practice principles enshrined in the actual legislation itself. The Mental Capacity Act 2005 begins with some categorical statements of principles in s. 1.

(2) A person must be assumed to have capacity unless it is established that he lacks capacity.
(3) A person is not to be treated as unable to make a decision unless all practicable steps to help him to do so have been taken without success.
(4) A person is not to be treated as unable to make a decision merely because he makes an unwise decision.

s. 1 Mental Capacity Act 2005

Professionals who make decisions on behalf of people who lack capacity must do so in their **best interests** (s. 1(5)) but before doing so must have regard to 'whether the purpose for which it is needed can be as effectively achieved in a way that is less restrictive of the person's rights and freedom of action' (s. 1(6)). Even when they do act in someone's best interests professionals continue to have an obligation to 'encourage the person to participate' in actions carried out or decisions made on their behalf (s. 4(4)). Clearly this implies taking into account their current wishes and feelings, and the beliefs and values they expressed when capable of doing so.

In effect capacity is defined in such a way that it is connected to the need to make a particular decision at a particular time and is always tied to the lack of ability to make a particular kind of decision at that time. Specifically the Act says:

s. 3(1)

… a person is unable to make a decision for himself if he is unable
(a) to understand information relevant to the decision,
(b) to retain the information,
(c) to use or weigh that information as part of the process of making the decision, or
(d) to communicate his decision (whether by talking, using sign language or any other means).

s. 3(1) Mental Capacity Act 2005

However, they are not to be regarded as unable to understand 'the information relevant to a decision' if they can understand an explanation provided in a way that is more appropriate, for example, 'using simple language, visual aids or any other means' (s. 3(2)). Furthermore, the fact that someone can only retain information for short periods of time does not prevent them 'from being regarded as able to make the decision' (s. 3(4)).

Thus the Mental Capacity Act 2005 clearly presents a definition of capacity, or rather lack of capacity, in such a way that minimizes the areas of a person's life which may be taken over by others and encapsulates in legislation what are in effect very sound social work principles of empowerment.

On-the-spot questions	1 What practice issues might arise from what s. 3 Mental Capacity Act 2005 says about capacity? 2 To what extent is the approach the law adopts consistent with principles of good social work practice?

Section 3 practice issues are explored further in this book in Chapter 3 and are well covered in ch. 3 of the *Mental Capacity Act 2005 Code of Practice* (Department for Constitutional Affairs, 2007) which includes some useful illustrative case examples. As to social work practice principles, it is clear that several of these – respect for individuals, empowerment, promoting independence, advancing human rights, for example – are entirely congruent although, as will be seen, there can be a potential conflict between promoting autonomy and preventing harm, neglect or abuse.

Conclusion

This chapter set out some very clear reasons why social workers need to know about the whole legal issue of capacity. Capacity centres, legally, around people's ability to make decisions for themselves and clearly is of crucial importance in social work practice both in relation to children and adults. The chapter included a brief overview of relevant legislation, underlining the importance in this area of considering common law and case law as well as what statute law actually says. For practice purposes some guidelines in legal judgments and various Codes of Practice will be helpful. Knowledge of this area of the law will greatly enhance the capacity of social workers to promote empowerment and to this end they will find it beneficial that parts of the legislation actually restate what are, in effect, some core social work principles and values. Throughout the rest of this book the focus is on examining ways in which different aspects of legislation can be put into practice in the context of empowering people to make decisions in as broad an area of their lives as is possible and thereby promote their autonomy.

Further reading

Adams, R (2008) *Empowerment, Participation and Social Work* offers a comprehensive overview of theories of empowerment. Chapter 5 focuses on empowering individuals with a range of examples of how this might apply to practice.

Social Care Institute for Excellence (SCIE) *Mental Capacity Act 2005 e-learning* www.scie.org.uk/publications/elearning/mentalcapacityact. This series of nine online tutorials, freely accessible to everyone, covers all the main provisions in the Mental Capacity Act 2005. Included are case studies and guidance on sound professional practice. The first tutorial, entitled *Supporting People to Make their Own Decisions*, is particularly recommended as an introduction and as a complement to this chapter.

Taylor, B (2010) *Professional Decision Making in Social Work Practice* is intended primarily for social workers post-qualifying. This book has a useful chapter 3 that focuses on decision-making in a legal context: consent, human rights and reasonable decisions in law.

1

WHAT CAN CHILDREN AND YOUNG PEOPLE DECIDE FOR THEMSELVES?

AT A GLANCE THIS CHAPTER COVERS:

- an outline of how the law approaches this question
- a case study that facilitates identification of the key relevant issues
- a summary of key judgments clarifying what the law says about young people's decision-making autonomy
- key connections with mental capacity law, child care law and mental health law
- a number of judgments made in actual cases

This chapter explains how the law enables children and young people to make decisions for themselves as they grow older. Instead of making a blanket assumption that no child or young person under 18 can make any decision about anything, the law has evolved to allow for the development of young people's capacity to make certain kinds of decisions as they grow older. It would be strange if no one under 18 could make any kind of decision yet suddenly on the attainment of their 18th birthday they acquired the capacity to make any decision they wished; and this is not how the law operates. However, this does raise substantive legal and ethical questions about the empowerment of children and young people. At what age, or by what criteria, can under-18s make decisions? What kind of decisions can they make? How should the law operate if young people make decisions that are objectively not in their interests? What should the role of professionals be and, crucially, to whom are they accountable – to parents who are legally responsible for their children, or to the child or young person themselves?

These are fundamental issues which this chapter begins to address. It will be seen that much of the law's response is through the development of case law, and the chapter assumes that readers are familiar with the role of case law in creating precedents, in interpreting legislation, and in providing guidance for those who are professionals engaged in work with children and young people. Hence this chapter is essential reading for all social workers, not just for those concerned with children and families. There are particular issues to do with 16 and 17-year-olds so even social workers who work in the field of mental health, indeed especially such social workers, need to be thoroughly familiar with these. It is assumed that social workers who work predominantly with children and families will already be familiar with the basic provisions of the Children Act 1989 and the general role of the courts in family proceedings.

The chapter works through a fictitious but true-to-life case study where there are issues of medical treatment, consent, social workers' powers, and the ability of young people to decide for themselves. Before introducing the case, and offering readers the opportunity of exploring different legal avenues, it is important to set out some of the key principles that apply to 16-year-olds, which incidentally also apply to 17-year-olds. It is worth noting in passing that 16 is an important milestone since it is the first age at which the law accords young people virtually full rights to decide for themselves.

Key principles

The law assumes adults have capacity and are competent to make decisions, but necessarily accepts that there are occasions in which people lose or partially lose capacity and this is covered generally by the Mental Capacity Act 2005, as explained in Chapter 1. Indeed, the *Mental Capacity Act 2005 Code of Practice* makes explicit what this 'presumption of capacity' is:

> The Act's starting point is to confirm in legislation that it should be assumed that an adult (aged 16 or over) has full legal capacity to make decisions for themselves (the right to autonomy) unless it can be shown that they lack capacity to make a decision for themselves at the time the decision needs to be made.
>
> *Department for Constitutional Affairs, 2007:15, para. 1.2*

The Mental Capacity Act 2005 can justifiably refer to age 16 since previous legislation has made it absolutely clear that 16 and 17-year-olds have the same right to consent and refuse medical treatment as adults who are now to be defined (by s. 1 Family Law Reform Act 1969) as people aged 18 or over.

s. 8 Consent by persons over 16 to surgical, medical and dental treatment.

(1) The consent of a minor who has attained the age of sixteen years to any surgical, medical or dental treatment which, in the absence of consent, would constitute a trespass to his person, shall be as effective as it would be if he were of full age; and where a minor has by virtue of this section given an effective consent to any treatment it shall not be necessary to obtain any consent for it from his parent or guardian.

(2) In this section 'surgical, medical or dental treatment' includes any procedure undertaken for the purposes of diagnosis, and this section applies to any procedure (including, in particular, the administration of an anaesthetic) which is ancillary to any treatment as it applies to that treatment.

Family Law Reform Act 1969

In the case of children and young people under 16, the extent to which they can consent to treatment will depend, crucially, on the extent to which the professional who is treating them or caring for them considers them able to understand and therefore decide for themselves. This principle arises from the judgment in the well-known '*Gillick*' case.

> **KEY CASE ANALYSIS**
>
> *Gillick v West Norfolk and Wisbech Area Health Authority* [1986]
>
> In this case a mother lost her attempt to get the courts to say that parents have the right of veto over the kind of treatment or medical advice given to under-16s. In this particular case there was an objection to girls under 16 receiving advice about contraception, which was overruled by the court, a decision confirmed in a subsequent similar case (*R (Axon) v The Secretary of State for Health and the Family Planning Association* [2006]) which concerned a parent's right to know if health care professionals proposed giving her children advice on sexual matters, including abortion. The court confirmed that parents did not have this right and went on to say that asserting young people's independent rights to confidentiality did not conflict with parental rights under Article 8 ECHR (right to family life and privacy).
>
> Lord Fraser, one of the judges who heard the *Gillick* case, set out a number of guidelines which would apply to a child under 16 who is considered to be of sufficient age and understanding to be competent to receive contraceptive advice without parental knowledge or consent. The health care professional must be satisfied that:
>
> - the young person will understand the advice;
> - the young person cannot be persuaded to tell his or her parents or allow the doctor to tell them that they are seeking contraceptive advice;
> - the young person is likely to begin or continue having unprotected sex with or without contraceptive treatment;
> - the young person's physical or mental health is likely to suffer unless he or she receives contraceptive advice or treatment.

Notwithstanding the fact that the *Gillick* and *Axon* cases both focused primarily on sexual health, it is generally agreed that the *Gillick* principles – capacity to make decisions increases in line with development, professionals decide whether to accept whether a young person is competent to give consent, professionals are then accountable to the 'competent' young person alone – are applicable much more widely and can relate to all kinds of medical treatment.

Overriding a 16-year-old's refusal to accept treatment

> ◤ **PRACTICE FOCUS**
>
> The parents of 16-year-old Abigail are despairing. She has anorexia nervosa and has lost so much weight that her life is in danger. Yet she still claims the absolute right to eat very little and says she knows what she is doing. The parents say that she cannot know and beg the professionals to intervene. What can be done?
>
> - Does Abigail have the absolute right to accept or refuse treatment or can her wishes be overridden in these circumstances and, if so, by whom?
> - What legislation is relevant here and in what way?
> - What difference would it make if Abigail were under 16?

Certainly a 'Gillick competent' younger Abigail could agree to treatment if she was considered to be 'capable of making a reasonable assessment of the advantages and disadvantages of the treatment proposed' (Lord Woolf in original judgment [1984] at 374–75). So in this Practice Focus example a 16-year-old Abigail could agree to treatment but that is not the problem here. Rather, she is refusing and her parents want to consent on her behalf. Section 8 of the Family Law Reform Act 1969 makes it quite clear that the right to agree to treatment passes to the 16-year-old. Yet does a 16-year-old have the absolute right to refuse treatment? For Abigail refusal may mean that her life is in danger, since in effect she is going to lose so much weight that this becomes life-threatening.

Perhaps the easiest way of addressing this question is to ask who could overrule her refusal and by what legal means might they be empowered to do so. The obvious first port of call is the parents. Could they overrule her?

Can parents simply override a young person's wishes?

On the face of it, the answer might appear to be no, since s. 8 Family Law Reform Act 1969 appears to give young people who are 16 or 17 the same rights as adults, and therefore by implication those rights would take over from the adult parents' right to consent on the young person's behalf. However, there is a need to distinguish between the legal right to give consent and an absolute right to refuse treatment. So it might be more accurate to say that consent is required for anyone under 18, and that consent can be provided either by a person with parental responsibility or by the young person themselves, if he or she is competent to do so. (For further consideration of the debates concerning this, see articles listed at the end of this chapter.)

This does, of course, raise a major ethical or practice dilemma. When would it be appropriate to override the consent of a competent young person, if at all?

On-the-spot question

Before reading further, draw up a list to answer the following question: in what situations might it be appropriate to override the consent of a competent young person?

This should by no means be confined to medical treatment but ought to cover, for example, agreements to participate in specific kinds of activities, in social work assessments, or in court proceedings.

Refusal to consent to medical treatment is an issue which has preoccupied the court in a number of very difficult cases. In *Re R* [1991] a 16-year-old girl refused treatment for anorexia nervosa, yet despite this and her being *Gillick* competent, the court ordered that she should be given drugs against her wishes. The court explicitly drew a distinction between the rights to give consent and the right to refuse, stating that if a young person refuses consent this did not stop other people such as parents consenting on their behalf.

The Court of Appeal came to a similar conclusion in *Re W (A Minor) (Medical Treatment)* [1992], a case that also concerned a 16-year-old with anorexia nervosa. In this case the girl being cared for by a local authority was admitted to a specialist adolescent residential unit. Because of concerns about her medical condition, the plan was to move her to a unit specializing in treating eating disorders, but the girl refused to go and refused to accept the planned medical treatment. In relation to the medical treatment there was an appeal against the judge's initial decision to override refusal. It was argued that if s. 8 Family Law Reform Act 1969 gave young people aged 16 and 17 the right to consent to medical treatment, and this was to be 'as effective as it would be if he were of full age', then that young person had an exclusive right to consent to such treatment and therefore an absolute right to refuse medical treatment because no one else would be in a position to consent. However, the Court of Appeal rejected that argument and overrode the refusal to accept treatment for anorexia.

The question of whether a young person's right to refuse treatment was absolute or could be overridden by someone with parental responsibility or by the court itself was considered in *Re B (A Minor) (Treatment and Secure Accommodation)* [1997]. In this case a 17-year-old who had a crack cocaine addiction, was pregnant and had refused treatment necessary to save both her own and the baby's lives. The court ruled that the young person did not have an absolute right to refuse; the right to refuse consent to medical treatment was an important factor but did not override the consent to treatment by someone who has parental responsibility for her or indeed consent by the court.

From these three cases it can be seen that, while the law gives 16 and 17-year-olds the right to give consent to medical treatment, case law has interpreted this to mean that this does not imply an absolute right to refuse treatment. Parents can give consent on behalf of young people, even when the young person refuses, and it is clear from these three and other cases that the courts will not hesitate to override consent where they deem it to be in the young person's interests to do so, particularly where the medical condition is life-threatening.

Can doctors simply override a young person's wishes?

What should happen if both the young person, who is capable of making their own decision, and those with parental responsibility refuse treatment? If courts have conceded the principle that someone with parental responsibility might override a 16 or 17-year-old's refusal, does this right to override extend to doctors? Here the answer seems clear that it does not and that, in cases where doctors are met with a refusal to accept medical treatment, then they must seek authority to override the consent.

Generally speaking courts have said that adults have an absolute right to refuse treatment if they have capacity. This principle has been established in a number of important cases, principally in *Re C (Adult: Refusal of Medical Treatment)* [1994] in which a psychiatric patient with a gangrenous leg refused treatment, and the court ruled that he was entitled to refuse the proposed amputation. Where cases involve young people under 18, doctors must approach someone with parental responsibility or, in difficult cases, the courts. Much depends on the extent to which the young person understands the nature of the treatment and for those under 16 the extent to which they are *Gillick* competent.

The case of *Re L (Medical Treatment: Gillick Competency)* [1998] considered this. Here, a 14-year-old practising Jehovah's Witness refused consent to medical treatment for extensive burns. She apparently feared that this might mean she would need a blood transfusion, and this was against her religion. However, the court held that the doctors had not fully explained the consequences of her refusal, particularly the kind of suffering she would experience which would lead to her death. For this reason the court was able to conclude that she did not have a full understanding of the decision and therefore her refusal should be overridden.

In a case which has some similarities, *Re E (A Minor)* [1993], the court overrode the refusal of a 15-year-old Jehovah's Witness to accept a blood transfusion for religious reasons. This appeared to be on the grounds that at 15 a young person does not understand the full consequences of their decisions and, specifically in this case, was unable to countenance the possibility of changing his views or his religious convictions. The judge commented: 'I respect this boy's profession of faith, but I cannot discount at least the possibility that he may in later life suffer some diminution in his convictions.' The decision in *Re M (A Child: Refusal of Medical Treatment)* [1999] revolved around the extent to which a 15-year-old girl's views were consistent. She simply refused to accept a heart transplant, despite the fact that she knew that this refusal might lead to her death, yet at the same time she clearly stated that she did not want to die. She did not appear to understand that that view was contradictory, and consequently the judge ruled that, while a refusal to accept treatment by a young person was an important factor in the case, it can never be decisive, and therefore the refusal was overruled.

On-the-spot question

The case law examples cited in this section have been primarily medical. Consider how they might potentially apply in a social work context. What situations might there be in social work where a young person has refused to give consent yet a social worker might wish to override this refusal by reference to a parent or even, exceptionally, the court?

One example might be where a young person refused to give information about someone who posed a threat to themselves or to other young people. Suppose that the young person then refused to agree to let information be recorded. The social worker would have to decide whether that would be an absolute right, or ought to be overridden if that information related to, say, abuse of another young person, or something equally serious.

How does the Mental Capacity Act 2005 apply in cases involving young people?

The Mental Capacity Act 2005 generally does not apply to under-16s, but does apply to 16 and 17-year-olds. All of the cases cited in the previous section occurred before the Mental Capacity Act 2005 came onto the statute book so the question arises as to whether, now that issues of capacity and consent are more clearly located within a statutory framework, this makes any difference?

In essence the Mental Capacity Act 2005 clarifies the kinds of decisions that can be made on someone else's behalf when someone does not have full capacity. However, certain kinds of decisions can never be made by individuals on behalf of other people. Section 27 of the Act lists these as: consent to marriage or civil partnership, sexual relations, divorce, dissolution of a civil partnership, consent to adoption, discharging parental responsibility to a child in some circumstances, and surrogacy. There may of course be circumstances in which those events might still happen: for example, s. 52 Adoption and Children Act 2002 permits courts to dispense with consent to an adoption order if the parent or guardian is 'incapable of giving consent'. Section 28 makes it plain that, despite being detained under the Mental Health Act 1983, a person does not lose their right to refuse treatment. Even in these circumstances the Mental Capacity Act 2005 does not allow treatment to be given to the patient without their consent, although there is some provision in the Mental Health Acts 1983 and 2007 for treatment against the patient's wishes (discussed later in this chapter). Section 29 prohibits voting on behalf of someone who has lost capacity and s. 62 prohibits any action in relation to assisted suicide.

It is worth noting in passing that the Mental Capacity Act 2005 also has provision in ss 24–26 to allow people to make advance decisions, which means that no one can give consent to certain kinds of treatment on their behalf, even when they lose capacity. However, this is not covered in detail in this chapter since provisions for making such decisions can only be made by someone aged 18 or above.

This then leaves a wide variety of decisions that can potentially be made on behalf of children and young people and normally, naturally, one would expect those decisions to be made by parents. However, as already seen, young people gradually acquire the potential to make decisions for themselves as they grow older and as they acquire *Gillick* competence. In effect the Mental Capacity Act 2005 makes little difference to that state of affairs. Case law indicates that, where consideration is given to overriding decisions made by 16 and 17-year-olds, this can be done simply by using principles established by relevant case law. This seems to indicate that the decision-maker needs to be either someone with parental responsibility or the court itself.

Decision-making powers of non-parents

As regards parental responsibility, remember that this can be someone other than a parent themselves. A person who has been granted a **residence order** under s. 8 Children Act 1989 also acquires parental responsibility in addition to anyone else who has it (s. 12(2) Children Act 1989). If a care order made under s. 31 Children Act 1989 is in force, the local authority also shares parental responsibility (s. 33 (3)(a) Children Act 1989) so could in theory make decisions on behalf of young people. So, next to consider is the special position of a local authority that shares parental responsibility with children and young people subject to care orders. This was considered in the next key case (see page 28) which concerns care proceedings and powers under interim care orders.

The decision in this case needs some explanation. It primarily concerns the extent to which a local authority gains the right to overrule young people's decisions when the authority is granted a court order under care proceedings. There have been other instances where local authorities have been pressurized to institute care proceedings in order to compel compliance with a course of action that appears to be in their long-term interests. In the 1980s for example, it was standard practice for courts to make care orders were the primary (and sometimes only) issue was that the young person was refusing to attend school. Similarly, care proceedings have been mooted in the past in cases where young people have refused to cooperate with assessments of their needs. The

> **KEY CASE ANALYSIS**

South Glamorgan County Council v W and B [1993]

The local authority went to court because it believed it was quite unable to do anything in the circumstances where a 15-year-old girl had barricaded herself into her father's house for 11 months. The local authority wanted to apply for an interim care order for the purpose of assessment, but the girl refused to cooperate. The local authority thought that she had the absolute right to refuse since s. 38(6) Children Act 1989 says that where the court makes an interim order it may give directions about medical examinations or assessments but that if the child is of 'sufficient understanding to make an informed decision' the child may refuse to submit to the examination or other assessment.

However, the judge declared that there were other considerations and that the court could interpret s. 100 Children Act 1989 so as to use its inherent jurisdiction in circumstances where there is reasonable cause to believe that if the court's inherent jurisdiction were not exercised the child will be likely to suffer significant harm (s. 100(4)(b) Children Act 1989). This can only be used where there is no other possible provision, such as an emergency protection order, but nevertheless does give the judge the right to order removal, assessment and, if necessary, treatment.

South Glamorgan case represents an extreme, but it was made absolutely clear in the judgment that the care order of itself did not give the local authority sweeping powers to override young people's rights to refuse to participate in assessments, although statute law clearly gives the local authority the right to say where the young person should reside (s. 33 Children Act 1989).

On-the-spot questions	Disregarding for the moment the significant ethical issues connected with using the law in this way: would care proceedings work as a means of compelling a young person to be admitted to a psychiatric resource?
	For example, in Abigail's case, could a local authority institute care proceedings in order to compel her to comply with a psychiatric placement?

Apart from the fact that this would hardly seem an appropriate course of action, there are two fundamental reasons why this would not be feasible.

First, it assumes that the grounds for care proceedings are fulfilled and that the court would be persuaded that a care order would be appropriate. The grounds for care proceedings stipulated in s. 31 Children Act 1989 are that the child is suffering, or is likely to suffer, 'significant harm' and that that harm is attributable to the care given to the child, or likely to be given if the order were not made, 'not being what it would be reasonable to expect a parent to give' or to the child or young person being 'beyond parental control' (s. 31(2) Children Act 1989; see also further reading at the end of this chapter). In this particular case, it seems unlikely that anyone would seek to prove that parents, who are manifestly worried sick about their daughter, were acting unreasonably or failing to provide care, given no indication of any lack of cooperation on the parents' part. It certainly seems inconceivable that anyone would be able to prove that she was beyond parental control. So this course of action seems highly questionable.

The second reason for rejecting this course of action is simply that a care order will not allow the local authority to do what is intended. Section 33 Children Act 1989 lists the powers that a local authority gains under a care order, principally to share parental responsibility and to keep the child or young person in their care (s. 33(1) and (3) Children Act 1989). A full reading of this section indicates that the local authority acquires no more rights than a parent already has, so it is difficult to see how a care order helps in any way whatsoever. Whilst there may be cases, exceptionally, where this would be an appropriate legal possibility, there are all sorts of ethical considerations and practice implications. For example, how would it be possible to work in the context in which there was constant friction and disputes between the local authority and the parents? This suggests that a more satisfactory way may be to request some kind of judicial decision concerning the medical treatment.

Effectively, that is what happened in the South Glamorgan case where the judge ruled that, in addition to an order under the Children Act 1989, it was also possible for the court to use its 'inherent jurisdiction' in certain exceptional circumstances. Use of these powers has also been made in other Children Act 1989 cases. In *Re C (A Minor) (Detention for Medical Treatment)* [1997] a 16-year-old girl refused treatment for anorexia and discharged herself from hospital. The court decided that it had inherent jurisdiction to take action in this case, specifically to order detention and treatment. The court declared that in such cases the welfare of the child was the court's paramount consideration, as is laid down in s. 1(1) Children Act 1989. In *Re W (A Minor) (Medical Treatment)* [1992] (already mentioned above) the local authority applied to the court under s. 100(3) and (4) Children Act 1989 for a direction that it was empowered to admit W to hospital for treatment without her consent if necessary. The judge decided that, although she had sufficient understanding to make an informed decision, the court could use its inherent jurisdiction powers and so authorized her removal to the specialist hospital and her treatment at it.

Returning to Abigail's case, all in all it looks as though pursuing care proceedings should be rejected as a potential course of action, not just on ethical grounds, but simply because it is very doubtful whether it would achieve its objective and in the vast majority of cases would simply not be feasible. That leaves one other potential course of legal action in Abigail's case: admission to hospital under the Mental Health Act 1983.

Would admission to hospital under mental health legislation be appropriate, with treatment under compulsion if necessary?

Part II Mental Health Act 1983 contains powers to apply for admission and detention in hospital, whilst Part IV of the Act covers consent to treatment which refers to powers to override patients' consent to treatment. This Act could potentially apply as there is no lower age limit, but the grounds for detention and criteria for overriding consent do need to be met. Note that overriding consent is only possible for patients who are detained, so the two actions would have to go in tandem, although they are separate procedures.

Compulsion only applies in relation to admission to hospital and treatment in hospital. The grounds for compulsory admission are set out in ss 2 and 3 Mental Health Act 1983. Section 2 stipulates that the 'patient' has to be 'suffering from mental disorder of a nature or degree which warrants the detention of the patient in a hospital for assessment' and ought to be detained in the interest of their own health and safety or for the protection of other people (s. 2). Section 3 is similar except that, being a longer-term order, it refers explicitly to a firm diagnosis of mental disorder and the necessity for treatment in hospital; 'appropriate medical treatment' must also be available (s. 3(2)(d)). It is questionable whether anorexia of itself is a mental disorder; decisions on this are purely clinical and need to be determined by doctors involved in the case. Once a detained patient is in hospital, s. 62 Mental Health Act 1983 allows for urgent treatment without the patient's consent, while s. 58 sets out the procedure to follow where patients refuse non-urgent treatment. In essence this involves referral to an independent psychiatric specialist who can authorize treatment without consent, unless the treatment falls under a narrow range of extreme treatments listed in s. 57 of the Act (for information on this see further reading at the end of this chapter).

So, in essence, as a legal procedure, if doctors agree that anorexia nervosa is a mental disorder, then there is potential for this to work in order to secure treatment against Abigail's wishes, but it does seem an extreme measure to adopt. It is a course of action to consider only in dire circumstances; there is some useful guidance on **proportionality** and what might constitute dire circumstances in case examples in the *Mental Capacity Act 2005 Code of Practice* (Department for Constitutional Affairs, 2007: ch. 13).

What difference would it make if someone were under 16?

Finally, a change of scenario to see whether it makes any difference if Abigail, in the Practice Focus example, were under 16. Strangely, the answer to this is that in effect there is not a lot of difference, despite the fact that s. 8 Family Law Reform Act 1969, in giving 16 and 17-year-olds the right to consent to medical treatment, appears to be distinguishing between their rights and those of under-16s.

One way of looking at this is to say that the law is about presumptions of capacity. If someone is 16 or over there is a legal presumption that they have capacity in this context. If they are under 16 there is a presumption that they do not. Both presumptions can be challenged by evidence presented to the court. If someone under 16 is regarded as having capacity then he or she is in the same position as a person aged 16 or over. However, in both cases, parents can also consent, a right the parents lose once someone attains the age of 18.

In interpretation the major difference appears to be that the younger the child or young person is, the more likely the court is to override their consent. However, in some cases courts have supported a child even though a parent has put forward strenuous objections to what the child has proposed to do. In *Re B (Wardship: Abortion)* [1991], a 12-year-old pregnant girl, supported by professionals and grandparents, wanted an abortion but the mother refused permission. The court decided in favour of the termination on the grounds that ultimately they were bound by the s. 1 Children Act 1989 principle that the welfare of the child was the 'paramount' consideration. In a much more recent case, there was a dispute between parents concerning a 10-year-old girl's choice of religion. In this case, *Re C (A Child)* [2012], the Jewish parents divorced and not long afterwards the father converted to Christianity whilst the mother continued to practise the Jewish faith. There was a shared care arrangement whereby the girl went to parents alternate weeks and while with the father she went to his church. Having attended church for some time she asked to be baptized as a Christian, a request that was met with strenuous objections by the mother who successfully obtained a prohibited steps order under s. 8 Children Act 1989. On appeal the court decided that the girl would be allowed to continue to explore baptism, despite the mother's objections, but was urged to wait. However, the court made it clear that if she decided she wanted to go through with baptism, the girl was entitled to do that despite the mother's opposition and objections.

Space does not permit more than a cursory examination of some of these fascinating cases, but readers interested in pursuing this will find a number of other cases discussed in the articles listed at the end of this chapter.

Conclusion

This chapter explored the principles which undergird the law relating to the capacity of young people under the age of 18. In essence the principle is developmental: children and young people acquire competence to make decisions for themselves as they grow older, but not in a linear sense which implies that capacity relates to chronological age, but rather as they become increasingly 'competent'. This principle relates to the influential judgment in the *Gillick* case and so has come to be known as *Gillick* competence. Sixteen and 17-year-olds have the right to consent to treatment, even against parental wishes, but case law suggests that this does not extend to the right to refuse treatment. In cases where children and young people appear to have made decisions which are not in their own interests, courts have taken on themselves the right to override those decisions, usually by adopting their inherent jurisdiction powers, and referring to the principle of paramountcy of the child's welfare contained in the Children Act 1989.

In cases which straddle the Children Act 1989, the Mental Capacity Act 2005 and the Mental Health Act 1983, much will depend on the precise circumstances of the case. Care proceedings would seem wholly inappropriate, and impossible unless the strict s. 31 Children Act 1989 criteria of 'significant harm' are met. The Mental Capacity Act 2005 itself, for the various reasons discussed in the chapter, appears to be of only marginal relevance. Of greater significance may be the provisions under the Mental Health Act 1983, although these require a clear clinical view that the young person potentially has a 'mental disorder' as defined in mental health legislation (for further discussion of what constitutes a mental disorder see Chapter 5). Ultimately, the High Court can cover those parts that statue law does not, and case law has demonstrated that judges are prepared to override refusals of young people to consent to treatment or care where the circumstances warrant it.

Further reading

Cave, E (2011) 'Maximization of minors' capacity' 23(4) *Child and Family Law Quarterly* 431–49: this article supports the case for extending Mental Capacity Act 2005 principles to under-16s, noting in particular that the Act's requirement to help people with impaired capacity to make competent decisions does not extend to that age group. The article argues that, nevertheless, there is a need to maximize the young person's capacity to consent and there is also a danger that 'paternalism will creep in through the back door'.

Chico, V and L Hagger (2011) 'The Mental Capacity Act 2005 and mature minors: a missed opportunity?' 33(2) *Journal of Social Welfare and Family Law* 157–68: this article analyses those cases where the courts have made decisions on behalf of young people. It argues that the Mental Capacity Act 2005 ought to have covered under-16s in cases where they appear to have the ability to make decisions for themselves. Included in the discussion is an overview of a number of interesting legal cases which are not covered in this chapter.

Gilmore, S and J Herring (2011) 'No is the hardest word: consent and children's autonomy' 23(1) *Child and Family Law Quarterly* 3–25: this article analyses a particular case in order to demonstrate that there is a distinction between a refusal to consent and a refusal to accept treatment. As a consequence in some cases a parent can have the power to consent, even where the child has refused. The article considers this, together with ethical arguments that would justify it.

Seymour, C and R Seymour (2013) *Practical Child Law for Social Workers*: an introduction to child care law written especially for students on qualifying programmes. This book offers an overview of law in relation to topics that are relevant to everyday social work practice, including a useful introductory chapter on rights.

2

HUMAN RIGHTS AND THE DEVELOPMENT OF LAW

AT A GLANCE THIS CHAPTER COVERS:

♦ where human rights law intersects with the law regarding capacity and empowerment
♦ relevant conventions of the ECHR
♦ key case concerning deprivation of liberty and passive consent
♦ the development of the Mental Capacity Act 2005 principles
♦ social workers' and other professionals' obligations

This chapter explores the connections between human rights law and the law in the UK as it applies to making decisions on behalf of vulnerable adults who are considered to have lost 'capacity' to make decisions for themselves. In this context, the term 'vulnerable adults' is quite wide-ranging so as to include people with mental health issues who are considered to pose a threat, either to themselves or other people. So, here the concern is not just with statutes concerning mental health and mental capacity, but also certain important common law principles that have historically allowed the courts to make decisions for other people when they consider this to be in their interests. Such common law provision claims long-standing historical pedigree, although, as will be seen, the European Court of Human Rights was not entirely happy with the way in which common law could be deployed in order to deprive people of their liberty.

The first part of this chapter is given over to an exploration of a key case where some fundamental issues concerning civil liberties and the role the courts came to the fore. The case assumes some familiarity with the differences between statute law and common law, so perhaps this would be a good point at which to recall the difference between law that is written down and law that is, in effect, created by the courts through an evolutionary process. Specific statute laws are considered alongside relevant Articles of the ECHR. This key case is generally referred to as '*Bournewood*'; it originally came to the courts in the UK as *R v Bournewood Community and Mental Health NHS Trust, ex parte L (Secretary of State for Health and Others Intervening)* [1998] but when it was taken to an appeal at the European Court became *HL v UK* [2004] (see page 37).

Human rights and capacity: the *Bournewood* case

Before discussing what happened in this case and addressing a number of related questions, some preliminary information concerning what the law says is needed. In addition, there may be one or two terms which are unfamiliar, so the discussion starts with those.

Best interests

The term 'best interests' refers to a long-standing belief that there is a general right to decide what should be done for people in circumstances where they are unable to make decisions for themselves, or where they have a condition that prevents them from making decisions themselves.

> **KEY CASE ANALYSIS**

HL v UK [2004]

The case concerned Mr L, a 49-year-old man with autism and learning disabilities, who, it was agreed, lacked capacity regarding certain kinds of decisions relevant to his care and treatment. He lived in the community with professional carers, who were the closest he had to any kind of immediate family.

He attended a day centre regularly, from which one day he was taken to hospital as a result of the behaviour he exhibited there. For about three months in 1997, Mr L was an inpatient at Bournewood Hospital. He was not detained under the Mental Health Act 1983; rather, he was accommodated in his own 'best interests' under the common law doctrine of 'necessity'. It was made clear to him and his carers that if he attempted to leave the hospital he would be detained under mental health legislation and to this end the hospital discouraged the carers from visiting for fear that Mr L would want to go home with them.

Mr L subsequently, through his carers, brought legal proceedings against the managers of the hospital, claiming that he had been unlawfully detained.

The High Court rejected the claim. It held that he had not, in fact, been detained, and that any detention would have been in his best interests and so lawful under the common law doctrine of necessity.

However, the Court of Appeal disagreed. It took the view that Mr L had been detained and that such detention would only have been lawful under the Mental Health Act 1983.

The House of Lords reversed this decision. It agreed with the High Court that the detention in hospital, being in Mr L's interests as determined by medical professionals and the court, was lawful. He did not have the capacity to understand his position; he did not actively object to being in hospital, and was not making any attempt to leave. The only issue was that his professional carers objected to him being there, believing that were he to return to their care, they could successfully manage his behaviour and he would not need to be in a psychiatric hospital.

At this point an appeal is made to the European Court, claiming that using the common law doctrine of necessity is a breach of the ECHR.

An obvious example is where someone is unconscious as a result of an accident. There is no doubt it is in that person's interest to be taken to hospital, so it is deemed unnecessary to have specific legislation that says that where a person is unconscious other people can act on their behalf. More controversially, it is assumed that there is a duty on professionals such as health care workers and social workers to prevent people harming themselves, so actively intervening to stop someone committing suicide is not only lawful, but expected. So, in this case it was argued that it was in Mr L's interests to be treated in a psychiatric hospital.

Common law doctrine of necessity

The common law doctrine of necessity in effect refers to the legal right to take steps that anyone could see are necessary for the good of others. A simple example is the right of firefighters to enter a burning building; no one would seriously suggest that they are committing an offence by breaking into a building in order to rescue people, save lives and prevent further damage to the building. By extension, the courts have argued that in some cases it is clear what needs to be done when the person concerned does not have the ability to give **active consent**. In a landmark case in 1989, *Re F (Mental Patient: Sterilisation)* [1990], the House of Lords extended the doctrine so that those who were treating someone who had lost capacity to consent would not be held guilty of an offence. In that specific case, doctors were allowed to avoid accusations of assaults by performing a sterilization without explicit, informed consent (Bartlett, 2007:27). In the *Bournewood* case, it was argued that preventing Mr L leaving hospital would not be an assault or an infringement of liberty because it was necessary for him to remain there.

Statute law: mental health

Mental health law makes provision for people who have a 'mental disorder' to be admitted to hospital and detained there even when they refuse to accept that they need inpatient care. Mental disorder is defined as 'any disorder or disability of the mind' but the relevant legislation then goes on to say that this specifically excludes 'dependence on alcohol or drugs'. Furthermore, a person with a 'learning disability' – legally defined as a 'state of arrested or incomplete development of the mind which includes significant impairment of intelligence and social functioning' – does not qualify as someone who is 'mentally disordered' unless their disability is 'associated with abnormally aggressive or seriously irresponsible conduct'

(s. 1 Mental Health Act 1983 as amended by Mental Health Act 2007). So this latter provision would prevent such a person being admitted to hospital under s. 3 Mental Health Act 1983 or being subject to guardianship under s. 7 of that Act.

Where someone is considered to have a 'mental disorder' and is in need of hospital admission, there are various provisions for compelling someone who refuses to agree to be admitted. Section 2 Mental Health Act 1983 allows for detention for up to 28-days maximum for assessment where someone is 'suffering from mental disorder of a nature or degree which warrants the detention of the patient in a hospital for assessment (or for assessment followed by medical treatment) for at least a limited period' and ought to be so detained in the interests of their own health or safety or with a view to the protection of other persons (s. 2(2)(a) Mental Health Act 1983). Section 3 allows for detention for treatment in hospital for a longer period (s. 20 of the Act says what this can be, generally maximum six months but renewable) where it is clear that someone does have a mental disorder, needs treatment in hospital which is available, and can only be dealt with in this way (see s. 3 Mental Health Act 1983 for precise wording of these conditions). Chapter 4 will explore some of this mental health legislation, and specifically its relationship to issues of capacity and consent, in more depth.

In order for these compulsory powers to be used there needs to be an application by an **Approved Mental Health Professional** or the '**nearest relative**' which is based on two independent medical recommendations (s. 12 Mental Health Act 1983). Once admitted, the person detained has a right to appeal to a tribunal (s. 66). These civil rights safeguards are important, not only for the obvious reason that they concern deprivation of liberty, but also to ensure that public law procedures comply with the rights to liberty expectations and the requirements of the ECHR.

The European Convention on Human Rights

The ECHR was formulated in the period just after the Second World War in an attempt to prevent a recurrence of the horrific outrageous abuse of fundamental rights that occurred in the Holocaust. European countries came together in the late 1940s to devise a series of fundamental rules that set down some markers or frameworks by which each country's own laws could be judged. The British government was instrumental in drawing up the Convention.

The ECHR includes a number of Articles: 14 key Articles, of which five are particularly relevant to this book:

Article 2	Right to life. Some general exemptions include execution as a court sentence; use of force in defence of someone subject to unlawful violence; lawful arrest or prevention of escape from custody; actions taken to quell a riot or insurrection.
Article 3	'No one shall be subjected to torture or to inhuman or degrading treatment or punishment.'
Article 5	Right to 'liberty and security of person'. General exceptions, in Article 5(1), include: (a) detention following conviction by court; (b) arrest and detention for non-compliance with law; (c) arrest or detention in order to bring before court on suspicion of committing offence; (d) detention of young people in relation to education; (e) 'the lawful detention of persons for the prevention of the spreading of infectious diseases, of persons of unsound mind, alcoholics or drug addicts, or vagrants'; (f) arrest in relation to deportation or extradition.
Article 6	Right to a fair trial
Article 8	Right to privacy and family life. Exceptions allowed if they are 'necessary in a democratic society in the interests of national security, public safety or the economic well-being of the country, for the prevention of disorder or crime, for the protection of health or morals, or for the protection of the rights and freedoms of others'.

Table 2.1: ECHR Articles

On-the-spot questions

1 In relation to each of these Articles how might they relate to issues relevant to social work practice with children?
2 In relation to each of these Articles how might they apply to issues relevant to social work practice with older people?

Here is a list of some quite contentious issues to which the Convention might relate (this list is by no means exhaustive and does not necessarily imply that Convention rights could be invoked in particular circumstances):

	Children	Older people
Article 2	Abortion	End of life care, assisted suicide
Article 3	Neglect, physical punishment	Quality of care in residential establishments
Article 5	Care orders	Forcible removal to care
Article 6	Appeals against adoption orders	Detention under mental health legislation
Article 8	Removal of children from parental care	Appealing decisions to close homes

Table 2.2: Contentious issues and the ECHR

Connecting the ECHR to the law

The Human Rights Act 1998 (s. 3) compels UK courts to take into account the ECHR in determining the outcome of all cases. It also compels Parliament to take the Convention into account when passing legislation and this also applies in retrospect in the sense that it provides a benchmark by which legislation is to be judged. It is open to the courts in the UK to declare that a particular law or decision is not compatible with the Convention, but courts do not have the right to strike down legislation, only to refer the matter back to Parliament for Parliament to consider what action to take.

The Human Rights Act 1998 (s. 6) compels public authorities, in exercising their duties, to take into account what the ECHR says. So a social worker or doctor who is employed by a public authority, such as social services or a health authority, must take the Convention into account when deciding whether and when to invoke mental health legislation. This is, of course, in addition to taking into account what the UK statute legislation says. So, for example, it is important to tell people of their rights to appeal to a tribunal, even if legislation does not specifically require this, since this could be a way in which people are empowered to use their rights under Article 6 which concerns rights to appeal to judicial authority concerning deprivation of liberty.

There are some limitations regarding how far the Convention can reach. Whilst the UK government generally implements the majority of decisions as they stand, there are no rules concerning when and how European Court decisions are implemented, or indeed the extent to which they are implemented (to quote a recent example, if the European

Court decides that prisoners have the right to vote it appears to be possible for the UK Parliament to implement this by only allowing certain categories of prisoners to vote). Also it may be worth noting that countries can opt out of specific provisions at the time a Convention is introduced, although not afterwards. This includes the right to refuse, or declare **reservations** about, amendments to Conventions. Furthermore, the Convention recognizes that each country will have slightly different interpretations, what is called the '**margin of appreciation**'. It also allows for 'reservation' of a very specific area where a country acknowledges that its laws do not conform to the Convention; and for '**derogation**' which permits non-compliance with the Convention in the event of public emergency.

Connecting the European Convention to mental health law

Of immediate relevance here is Article 5 concerning liberty, and this connects to mental health practice and legislation in three specific areas:

1 To what extent and how can compulsory intervention powers, laws requiring people to be deprived of liberty in hospital, be considered compatible with the ECHR?
2 What safeguards would the Convention expect to exist in order to protect people's fundamental rights with regard to admission to hospital?
3 How does the Convention relate to people being detained in hospital once they are admitted?

The key Convention Article here is Article 5 concerning the right to liberty and 'security of person'. Article 5(1)(e) permits provisions for 'laws for detention of ... persons of unsound mind' among others.

The question then is not what does unsound mind actually mean, but rather who decides and in what circumstances? (See page 43.)

In determining whether someone has a mental disorder, and a disorder of the kind or degree that justified deprivation of liberty, the European Court expected this to be decided by someone who has clinical or professional knowledge. In the Dutch case before it, the decision was made by a relative and a local mayor, neither of whom could really claim clinical competence in the diagnosis of mental disorder. In addition, there need to be stipulated reasons as to why someone has to be kept in hospital, once they are admitted. The maximum period that mental health legislation allows for detention is not meant to be a minimum, in

> **KEY CASE ANALYSIS**

Winterwerp v The Netherlands [1979]

Fundamentally, the Convention asks: what are fair procedures which determine whether someone is 'of unsound mind'? This key European court case laid down procedures and principles that would be applied to all future mental health cases. These are:

- the existence of a mental disorder must be verified;
- the mental disorder must be of a kind or degree wanting compulsory confinement; and
- the validity of continued confinement has to be justified.

other words, it is not a sentence. It must therefore be possible for someone to appeal to an independent body where they consider that they no longer need to be detained.

A separate case, *Megyeri v Germany* [1992], established that the procedure for reviewing continued detention had to be quasi-judicial. In other words, not only did there have to be a process whereby someone detained could have their case reviewed, such a process would need to conform to legal requirements regarding such matters as evidence and the general principles of fair trial. Crucially, detained patients were entitled to regular reviews of their case without having to take the initiative.

Applying the ECHR to the *Bournewood* case

Given the provisions in the ECHR and mental health law governing compulsory intervention, it should now be possible to try to see how the actions taken in the *Bournewood* case match with the Convention and deprivation of liberty law.

Perhaps predictably, outside of mental health law there is no general legislation that allows for people to be deprived of their liberty. There is a rarely used public health provision that permits the removal of someone 'suffering from grave chronic disease or, being aged, infirm or physically incapacitated' who is living in 'insanitary conditions' and not receiving 'proper care and attention' (s. 47 National Assistance Act 1948). This law is generally regarded as something of an anachronism, incompatible with Article 5 ECHR, and there are moves to abolish it, strongly endorsed by the Law Commission (Law Commission, 2011:

para. 973). There is a very specific police power to enter and search premises in the case of 'life and limb' but this is strictly for emergency use only (s. 17 (1) Police and Criminal Evidence Act 1984). With these two specific exceptions, the law concerning overriding consent for people who do not, temporarily or permanently, appear to have capacity is confined to law addressed here relating to mental health and mental capacity.

Returning to the *Bournewood* key case, *HL v UK* [2004] summarized above, this can now be measured against the legal yardsticks that have just been outlined. There are a number of important considerations:

- which ECHR Articles the actions taken in this case might have breached;
- how actions breached those Articles; and
- the implications of ruling that the actions taken were contrary to the ECHR.

The answer to the first two questions is to be found in the summary of the European Court's decision that now follows. After this, the implications of the European Court's ruling are discussed.

The European court's decision in the *Bournewood* case

The European Court allowed the appeal by Mr L and his carers. In essence, the European Court of Human Rights agreed with the Court of Appeal since it found that Mr L had been detained, so that the 'right to liberty' in Article 5 ECHR was relevant. Furthermore, the court held that detention under the common law was incompatible with Article 5 because common law was 'too arbitrary' and 'lacked sufficient safeguards', specifically the kind of safeguards that were available to patients detained under the Mental Health Act 1983.

The European Court of Human Rights also held that judicial review, the only way Mr L had been able to challenge his common law detention, did not provide the kind of rigorous challenge required by Article 5(4) ECHR. In this sense the actions taken breached Article 6.

So there was a breach of Articles 5 and 6.

The finding of the court that detention had taken place is important when considering whether people have to give active or **passive consent**. Consent is covered in more detail in chapter 3 as it requires a thorough discussion, for a real concern to some practitioners is that people can have their rights accidentally disregarded simply because they do not strenuously object to what is going on. In this particular case Mr L was compliant with the actions taken by staff who removed him from the day centre to the hospital, and who then told him that he had to remain in the hospital. Nevertheless, the European Court decided that this compliance could not be taken as consent. Having decided that Mr L lacks capacity in relation to the decision about whether he ought to go to hospital, the public authorities cannot then assume consent on his behalf because he did not demonstrate objection. What was needed was some clarity in the law, so that it became clear who was taking the decision on his behalf, and what specific explicit reasons they had for determining that he ought to stay in hospital.

In answer to the question about who was making the decision on behalf of Mr L, whilst theoretically this ought to have been the UK court, the absence of a legal order meant that it was unclear who made the decision and on what grounds. Here the European Court said that the court failed to give proper regard to what the Convention expected in terms of how patients could object to detention and what processes exist for ensuring that their deprivation could be reviewed. Had Mr L been detained under the Mental Health Act 1983 it was clear what procedure would apply: written records of two medical recommendations and a formal application made by someone with authority to do so. Detention would have been for a specified maximum period and, during this time, Mr L and his carers would have had the right to object to the tribunal, which could have discharged him from the order, or would have had to declare firm grounds for overriding his consent if it had chosen not to discharge him. All of this matches the approach to Article 6 set out in the principles declared in the *Winterwerp* key case discussed above.

The implications of the European Court's decision

The implications can be summarized very concisely: the European Court identified a gap, which became popularly known as the '***Bournewood gap***'. This can best be demonstrated by a diagram (see next page) that reflects the law as it was at the time of the *Bournewood* judgment.

How to address this gap proved challenging, but by the time the European Court's decision was announced in 2004, there had already been a number of reviews of the law relating to capacity and vulnerable

Area of law	Children and young people	Learning disabilities, vulnerable adults	Mental health
Who decides?	Parents or young person themselves	Professionals involved in care	Approved doctors, Approved Mental Health Professionals
Which law says so?	Family Law Reform Act 1969; Children Act 1989	*Bournewood* gap	Mental Health Act 1983
How is law interpreted?	Courts have clear role in family proceedings; case law, especially the *Gillick* case discussed in chapter 1	By reference to criteria that evolved over time, common law, various legal doctrines (see discussion above)	Professionals apply statutory criteria, subject to review by hospital managers and appeal procedures
How can decisions be challenged?	Appeal courts, judicial review	Only by judicial review	By appeal to the first-tier tribunal

Table 2.3: Law at the time of the *Bournewood* judgment

adults. The Law Commission, which has a responsibility to review and reform areas of the law at the request of Parliament, produced proposals in 1993 (Law Commission, 1993). These were followed by proposals from the Lord Chancellor (Lord Chancellor's Department, 1997; 1999). Parliament had already begun to review the law in this area, having taken soundings from a variety of professional bodies, and this culminated in the passage of the Mental Capacity Act 2005 which puts onto a statutory footing a number of key principles in relation to capacity and empowerment. Chief amongst these is the notion of 'best interests' which relates to decision-making on behalf of people who have temporarily or permanently lost capacity in relation to one specific area of decision-making (s. 4 Mental Capacity Act 2005).

So one very obvious way of plugging the *Bournewood* gap would simply be to use the Mental Capacity Act 2005 as a means of addressing the European Court's reservations about UK law, and this is precisely what happened. However, the Mental Capacity Act 2005 as it was originally formulated did not quite match all the requirements and issues identified by the European Court, so fairly soon after the Mental Capacity

Act 2005 was passed it had to be amended by the Mental Health Act 2007 in order to bring it fully into line with the ECHR.

The crucial issues that the Mental Capacity Act 2005 failed to address were:

- Who should be the decision-makers and, crucially, what qualifications would they have to make major decisions over other people's lives when these involve Article 5 relating to liberty?
- What avenues of redress or appeal are open to people who are deprived of their rights under the ECHR, specifically their right to liberty which was the issue in the *Bournewood* case?

Specific measures were subsequently introduced to address these questions through precise requirements relating to s. 4 Mental Capacity Act 2005 which concerns the whole notion of best interests. There are now two additional sections, ss 4A and 4B, that specifically address the whole issue of deprivation of liberty in the context of mental capacity. These sections refer in turn to a Schedule and related regulations, which cover the identification and training of decision-makers, the procedures by which someone can be deprived of their liberty when they lack capacity, and the rights to appeal such decisions. As this is such an important topic, it merits consideration in a separate chapter (Chapter 5).

So for now simply note that the *Bournewood* gap has been filled as shown in Table 2.4 (see top of page 48).

Applying the ECHR to issues of capacity: case law examples

Having explored the key case that raised the whole issue of the inadequacy of legal safeguards prior to 2005, this chapter now goes on to consider a couple of examples where the Convention may also apply, focusing on cases that are particularly relevant to social work practice.

Parents with learning disabilities

It is easy to fall into the trap of thinking that there are two sets of laws that apply to social work: those that apply to adult social care, such as the National Health Service and Community Care Act 1990, the National Assistance Act 1948, or the Mental Capacity Act 2005, and those that apply to childcare, such as the Children Act 1989, Adoption and Children Act 2002, Children and Young Persons Act 2008. However, in some important contexts, adult care social workers need to know about

Area of law	Children and young people	Learning disabilities, vulnerable adults	Mental health
Who decides?	Parents or young person themselves	Professionals involved in care	Approved doctors, Approved Mental Health Professionals
Which law says so?	Family Law Reform Act; 1969; Children Act 1989	Mental Capacity Act 2005 as amended by s. 50 Mental Health Act 2007	Mental Health Act 1983
How is law interpreted?	Courts have clear role in family proceedings; case law, especially the *Gillick* case discussed in chapter 1	By reference to criteria that evolved over time, common law, various legal doctrines, but now also case law relating to amended Mental Capacity Act 2005	Professionals apply statutory criteria, subject to review by hospital managers and appeal procedures
How can decisions be challenged?	Appeal courts, judicial review	Only by judicial review unless Deprivation of Liberty Safeguards apply in which there is a formal review process	By appeal to the first-tier tribunal

Table 2.4: Law after implementation of legislative reforms necessitated by the *Bournewood* judgment

child care law and conversely, here, child care social workers need to know about the Mental Capacity Act 2005 especially when addressing child protection issues with parents with learning disabilities. There are, of course, other circumstances, such as, for example, what happens when very young parents, who are themselves technically minors, have to make decisions about their children (see further reading at the end of this chapter).

The Mental Capacity Act 2005 generally applies to everyone aged 16 or above (although it also covers under-16s in the context of ill-treatment) and this includes, obviously, parents with learning disabilities. The obligations under the Act, which will be examined in more detail in the next chapter, revolve around empowering people to make decisions to the extent that they are able to do so, including cases where people have **'fluctuating capacity'** (ss 2 and 3 Mental Capacity Act 2005).

There is also a statutory obligation under the Human Rights Act 1998 for local authorities to ensure that their actions are compliant with the ECHR and, in this context, in particular Article 8 concerning rights to family life. This means, quite emphatically, that it is not lawful for social workers simply to assume that because parents have learning disabilities they potentially pose a threat to their children, or ignore this factor in formulating child protection plans. Both the Mental Capacity Act 2005 and the ECHR say otherwise.

> **KEY CASE ANALYSIS**

Coventry City Council v C and Others [2012]

Baby C was the mother's fourth child, all three previous children having been placed for adoption. The judge made it clear that the mother had never harmed any of her children and had always co-operated with everyone trying to help her. Nevertheless, it was generally agreed that she had significant learning difficulties and, while she could manage well under supervised contact, appeared to have no 'instinctive or intuitive feel for parenting'. Because of this, the local authority plan was to remove the newborn baby as soon as the mother was discharged from hospital, and the mother appeared to consent to this, or rather did not object.

At the time of the birth, there were medical complications and the mother needed life-sustaining surgery. She was offered accommodation for her baby under s. 20 Children Act 1989, which initially she refused. However, once she had been treated with morphine, she agreed.

The legal issues were twofold:

1 Did the local authority respect Article 8 ECHR?
2 Was this a valid consent since there were clearly questions about whether the mother had capacity?

The local authority conceded that removing the child at birth was not 'proportionate', this being the criterion for determining whether local authorities can lawfully breach parents' rights to look after their own children. Actions would need to be proportionate to the potential risk to the child, which would have to be of such a high order that there would really be no other alternative.

As regards capacity, the court made it clear that it was not acceptable for the social worker to say that the mother had given consent to her child being accommodated under s. 20, since there were clear reasons as to why she could not be regarded as having capacity to do so.

Criticism of support services for parents with learning disabilities and actions taken in care proceedings cases have centred on negative assumptions about those parents' potential for parenting. There can be an assumption that the learning disability of itself equates with the inability to parent and, likewise, that any perceived shortcoming is attributable to that learning disability (SCIE, 2005; MacIntyre and Stewart, 2011). This is confounded by the success of projects designed to support parents with learning disabilities who are involved with child protection services (Tarleton and Porter, 2012). Nevertheless, the proportion of parents with learning disabilities in care proceedings is significant: Booth and Booth (2004) found that one-sixth of care proceedings in one particular local authority involved a parent with a learning disability and, perhaps more significantly, in three-quarters of these cases children were removed. A subsequent article (Booth et al., 2006) argued that parents with learning disabilities were on the receiving end of 'temporal discrimination' and referred to the legal system mitigating against parents with learning disabilities who were trying to hold on to children being considered for adoption.

These issues came to the fore in a care proceedings case decided by the courts in 2012 (see page 49). In addition there was a major issue concerning capacity.

In this particular case, the court concluded that the social worker had effectively misled the parent by reassuring her that removal was a temporary arrangement when in reality the social worker knew that it was extremely unlikely that the child would be returned. In future cases, the court suggested that social workers should follow these guidelines:

1 They must satisfy themselves that the person giving consent has capacity and that they do not temporarily lack capacity.
2 In considering consent, the social worker must actively address the questions raised by s. 3 Mental Capacity Act 2005, especially the ability to evaluate information.
3 Obtaining parental consent in particular circumstances and contexts has to be fair and proportionate.
4 Consent, if given, must be fully informed. This means that the parent must:

   a. understand the consequences of giving consent;
   b. appreciate the range of choices available;
   c. possess all the facts relevant to that consent.

5   If the social worker has doubts about capacity no further attempt should be made to obtain consent and advice should be sought.

6   Even if social workers are satisfied that consent is fully informed, they must then consider whether the action taken in accommodating the child is both fair and proportionate.

7   It may also be relevant to consider the physical and psychological state of the parent, whether they are currently receiving legal advice or the advice of relatives, whether it is necessary for the safety of the child to be separated from the mother at this particular time, and finally whether it would be fairer for the case to be brought before the court.

8   In short, local authorities should approach obtaining s. 20 agreements at the point of birth with great caution and care, especially where there is no immediate danger and the local authority would be unlikely to obtain a court order.

This case is a salutary lesson for social workers involved in difficult and often harrowing cases where children are removed at birth, and where they are tempted to offer false reassurance. Courts will rightly insist that social workers are totally honest with parents, since in this case it could be suggested that the social worker took advantage of the situation where a parent was receiving medical treatment in order to secure apparent cooperation. If nothing else, this case underlines the importance of being aware of legal requirements concerning capacity and decision-making, of which more in the next chapter.

Safeguarding vulnerable adults

The next case concerns safeguarding vulnerable adults and the extent to which the local authority is entitled to take decisions that apparently fly in the face of people's Article 8 ECHR rights to family life. In this case a well-meaning local authority tried to protect a woman who had vascular dementia from a man with whom she had formed a close relationship. They did this by banning 'S' from visiting 'M' whom they considered had lost capacity and therefore may have been unable to appreciate ways in which S may have been trying to exploit the relationship.

> **KEY CASE ANALYSIS**

Re MM [2009]

There was no doubt that the close relationship between M and S meant that they could be considered to have a right to family life under Article 8. The relationship was both physical and emotional.

M's relatives became concerned that the visits were causing distress and so involved the local authority which tried to find out what exactly M wanted. A meeting was held at which it was decided that M's capacity needed to be assessed in order to determine whether she was able to agree to visits, or whether one of her relatives (D) should have the authority to make that decision on her behalf.

Whilst the medical assessment capacity was being arranged, D informed S that she was not allowing him to visit M. Despite a complaint from S, the local authority took 10 months to arrange the assessment of M's capacity, during which time no contact took place between them. When the assessment was made, it suggested that contact should be allowed but only if supervised. This was later confirmed as appropriate by the Court of Protection.

S applied to the court for a declaration that the delay in obtaining a capacity assessment meant that his fundamental rights under Article 8 had been breached.

The court agreed that the Convention had been breached. Specifically, the court said that the local authority should have acted much more quickly in assessing capacity since delay could of itself amount to infringement of fundamental human rights. The local authority and the care home were wrong to allow D to make decisions on behalf of M. What they should have done is acted on M's last known wish expressed at a time when she did have capacity.

In simply going along with what D said, the local authority had failed to make an overall judgment about what was in M's best interests, as was required by the Mental Capacity Act 2005. Also it did not appear to have considered whether the actions taken were proportionate, as was required when interpreting Article 8.

In this case, the lengthy delay in obtaining the assessment of mental capacity meant that, inevitably, the court had to decide that there was a breach of this couple's right to family life. It may, on the surface appear odd to ban people who clearly are in a relationship from seeing each other, but if the local authority truly believed that one of them was a vulnerable adult at risk of sexual, financial or other forms of exploitation, it would have a responsibility under safeguarding procedures to adopt a protective course of action. As a preliminary step, it would clearly need to know for certain that the vulnerable adult had lost capacity in relation to decisions about sexual activity, financial matters and risks generally. Once having determined that, the local authority would only be justified in acting if there was clear evidence of capacity having been lost. If there is any doubt, then the local authority must ensure that actions are based on the last known wishes of the vulnerable adult. The next chapter discusses further how some of these principles related to the Mental Capacity Act 2005 operate, but this case is a useful reminder that safeguarding action needs to connect not just to the Mental Capacity Act 2005 but must, above all, comply with the overall requirements of the ECHR.

Social workers' obligations under human rights legislation

So far, this chapter has explored ways in which the law relating to capacity and empowerment has developed in the light of the incorporation of the ECHR into UK law. This led to consideration of a key case, *Bournewood*, that influenced the reformulation of the law regarding vulnerable adults. Also considered was how the Convention applies to parents who have learning disabilities where the key question is whether someone has the capacity to consent at a critical time in their lives. The case also raised fundamental questions about empowerment and disempowerment in the context of child protection. Likewise, in adult safeguarding cases, social workers need to be careful about allowing actions to be taken that on the surface appear to be empowering vulnerable adults, but may inadvertently trammel the Convention rights of others.

It may come as surprise to learn that the obligation to comply with the European Convention does not apply in every situation. Case law has established, for example, that residents who wished to complain of a breach of Article 8 had to satisfy the court that the service provider was under an obligation to comply with the Article. In 2001, a case concerning a decision by the Leonard Cheshire foundation to close a residential home could not be challenged on these grounds as the service provider was a voluntary organization, not a local authority (*Heather Ward and Callin v Leonard Cheshire Foundation and HM Attorney-General* [2001]). This is because the Human Rights Act 1998, which incorporated the Convention into UK law, applies to 'public authorities' (s. 6 Human

Rights Act 1998) and the court held that this did not include voluntary organizations and charities. In 2007, the House of Lords ruled that the Human Rights Act 1998 does not even extend to people whose accommodation in private care homes is funded by the local authority (*YL v Birmingham City Council* [2007]). However, this decision was effectively reversed by Parliament by statute law: s. 145 Health and Social Care Act 2008. Nevertheless, courts still have to consider whether **organizations** are '**hybrid**' in that they exercise both public and private functions (*London & Quadrant Housing Trust v R* [2009]).

Conclusion

> *On-the-spot question*
>
> So, finally, by way of revising what is in this chapter, why must practitioners pay particular attention to the Convention?

There are a whole number of reasons, apart from the obvious one that there is a legal obligation to do so. Hopefully, readers' reflections will have suggested at least some of the answers that follow, and maybe a few others as well, as this list is not meant to be exhaustive.

1 Human rights conventions set out broad frameworks that regulate the relationship between individuals and the state, important in social work where in some instances compulsory intervention is sanctioned by law.
2 To this end, human rights conventions offer criteria by which the laws that permit social workers to intervene directly in families are themselves held up to scrutiny.
3 In this connection, human rights conventions offer a means of scrutinizing the decisions which social workers make when carrying out their duties under that legislation.
4 In effect what this means is that human rights considerations intersect law and decision-making, enabling fundamental questions to be asked such as: is the action proportionate, does it correctly balance needs of children with rights of parents, does it fully respect people's ability to make decisions themselves, at least in some regards?
5 Human rights legislation is by definition a form of empowerment, offering valuable means of redress, with international arbitrators.

6 As far as the court system is concerned, the European Court itself offers an additional Court of Appeal, over and above what is offered within the UK court system.

7 Decisions in human rights cases can strengthen the argument for additional legal safeguards, as was demonstrated in the *Bournewood* case.

8 Decisions on human rights cases can expose practice that undermines or infringes basic rights.

9 Decisions in the human rights cases therefore offer some guidance about balancing rights.

10 Human rights-related law starts from the presumption that people should be as free as possible and should be empowered to make their own choices and decisions, so is consistent with core social work principles and values.

Further reading

Fovargue, S (2013) 'Doctrinal incoherence or practical problem? Minor parents consenting to their offspring's medical treatment and involvement in research in England and Wales' 25(1) *Child and Family Law Quarterly* 1–18. This article explores how the law applies in the situation where parents are under 18. The argument put forward is that the law is incoherent and rather confused in this area and what is needed is clarity about young parents' capacity to make decisions and, for those under 16, the appointment of 'supportive guardians' who would be empowered to make decisions on behalf of very young parents.

Freeman, M (2011) *Human Rights*: a useful introduction to human rights and ways in which human rights are safeguarded through legal means. This book adopts a critical and challenging approach and is particularly strong on theories of rights and human rights in relation to minority groups, who in this context include children.

Law Commission (2011) *Adult Social Care* is a comprehensive review of adult care law that produced a welter of recommendations for reforming the law relating to adult care. It came up with what it claims to be 'the most far-reaching reforms of adult social care law seen for over 60 years'. Most of them were accepted by government and are therefore planned to feature in future legislation on adult care, especially safeguarding.

Manthorpe, J, J Rapaport and N Stanley (2008) 'The Mental Capacity Act 2005 and its influences on social work practice: debate and synthesis' 20(3) *Practice* 151–62. Written at a time when the Act was newly implemented, this article outlines the scope of the Mental Capacity Act 2005 and considers the implications of the Act for social work practice. It is particularly useful for its summary of historical background and examination of the Mental Capacity Act 2005 in a social work context.

McDonald, A (2007) 'The impact of the UK Human Rights Act 1998 on decision making in adult social care in England and Wales' 1(1) *Ethics and Social Welfare* 76–94. This article offers a sound overview of how the Human Rights Act 1998 impacts on adult social care law with an emphasis on a theoretical discussion of rights which will extend the basic introduction to rights set out in this chapter.

McGhee, J and S Hunter (2011) 'The Scottish children's hearings tribunals system: a better forum for parents with learning disabilities?' 33(3) *Journal of Social Welfare and Family Law* 255–66. This article extends the discussion above concerning over-representation of parents with learning disabilities in care proceedings cases. It explores whether the Scottish children's hearings tribunal system offers a model that is more responsive to the needs of parents with learning disabilities, and whether they are empowered to participate more effectively in cases concerning their children's welfare.

3

THE MENTAL CAPACITY ACT 2005 PRINCIPLES

AT A GLANCE THIS CHAPTER COVERS:

- principles relating to capacity and consent
- how the principles laid down in the Mental Capacity Act 2005 apply in practice
- how the courts say capacity should be assessed when there are doubts about people's ability to make their own decisions
- advance decisions

This chapter identifies a number of key principles underpinning the Mental Capacity Act 2005 and then goes on to explore how these might apply in fairly typical scenarios. The core principles were summarized briefly at the end of Chapter 2 but here they are explored in more detail, paying attention to how they may apply in practice.

These principles fall under various headings. A preliminary step is to clarify what is meant by consent, and here specifically addressed is the distinction between active (expressed) and passive (implied) consent since this highlights a principle underlying the Mental Capacity Act 2005 that some circumstances ordinarily and routinely justify decisions being made on behalf of other people. The discussion then centres on the Mental Capacity Act 2005 itself beginning with the fundamental question: to whom does the Mental Capacity Act 2005 apply? Who can be considered to have lost the capacity as interpreted under the Mental Capacity Act 2005? There is some guidance from courts on this and a couple of examples from relevant case law will be highlighted below. Next in this chapter comes a broader consideration of the issue of empowerment, which incorporates the important notion of 'best interests' which is highlighted by the Act, and which will be discussed further in chapter 5 in relation to the Deprivation of Liberty Safeguards introduced by the Mental Health Act 2007. Finally, this chapter considers the range of decisions that people can make for themselves in advance – something many people might want to do since there is always the possibility in everyone's life that at some stage they will become incapacitated. In those circumstances how can someone ensure that their wishes are fulfilled? The law is quite clear about the kinds of decisions that can and cannot be made in advance and how people can have their wishes acted upon when they are no longer able to contribute to the decision-making process.

In this area, case law is of particular importance, and a number of relevant cases will be summarized in this and subsequent chapters. However, by its very nature, case law develops all the time so it would be prudent for practitioners in this area to find out how to keep up to date with developments. University students may be able to access one of the legal databases, such as Lexis or Lawtel through their library. Not quite as authoritative, but more accessible, are a number of sources accessible through the internet. Alternatively, or in addition, it is possible to subscribe to an online community of interest. Within social work agencies there are groups of practitioners who work in a particular field who meet regularly and, of course, nothing substitutes for attending regular training sessions to keep up to date with practice and legislation. For some practitioners, such as Approved Mental Health Professionals or Deprivation of Liberty Safeguards **Best Interests Assessors** (BIAs), attending such sessions is a requirement of one of the regulatory bodies: respectively the HCPC and The College of Social Work (TCSW).

Assumed consent

Although not specifically addressed in the Mental Capacity Act 2005, it is clear that one of the principal purposes of the Act is to extend the reach of legislation so as to include protection for people where it is doubtful whether they give consent or not. In other words, it is not simply about procedures for overriding people's right to make decisions where they actively refuse consent. It also concerns passive consent.

One simple way of distinguishing active and passive (assumed) consent is to say that active consent involves an explicit statement from someone that they agree to a course of action. At its very basic, it is simply someone saying 'yes'. Passive assumed consent is more problematic, and is sometimes a real concern in social work.

Sometimes it may be obvious that people should act on the basis of passive consent. For example, consider the following circumstances:

On-the-spot questions	In each of these scenarios consider whether consent can be assumed. 1 A mountaineer loses his footing at the top of the mountain and falls several feet, and lies unconscious. He is rescued by the mountain rescue team and taken to hospital. At no point is the mountaineer asked if he wishes to go to hospital, or whether he wishes to be treated when he arrives there since he is still unconscious. 2 When the meals on wheels volunteer cannot gain entry to Mrs Smith's house, they summon assistance and, on entering the back door, find Mrs Smith lying semi-conscious on the floor. They call an ambulance and she has is taken to hospital where, despite the fact that she can communicate, no one asks whether she agrees to be treated for the injuries she sustained in the fall.

On-the-spot questions

3 The mountaineer regains consciousness and needs to be treated for a broken leg. Medical staff ask him to sign to say he agrees to having his leg set in plaster.
4 Mrs Smith is told she needs to be kept in hospital overnight. She says she wants to go home and she is worried about her cat, but medical staff tell her that she must stay as it is possible she has concussion after her fall.

In the first example, it is obvious why someone cannot give consent and why it is reasonable for the law to assume that people can be treated in these circumstances. It is, as it were, common sense, but it is also common law. There is a clear undergirding principle that life should be preserved and that people should be treated when they are in danger. Very few would argue with that, although one could debate whether this is an ethical or a legal principle.

This becomes more apparent in the second scenario. Here the action of entering the house once it is realized that someone is semi-conscious would be defensible, but somewhat more questionable is treating someone for their injuries without asking them even though they clearly can communicate. Nevertheless, it could be argued that the assumption that someone would want to be treated in these circumstances is reasonable, until such time as the person receiving treatment indicated an objection. Both these examples are of passive consent where consent has been assumed.

In the third scenario, which requires active intervention by medical staff in a situation where someone can be asked, it is again obvious why they would do so and in this case consent would need to be quite explicit, and probably written down. This is clearly a case where active consent is required.

The fourth case is fairly typical of the kind of scenario which social workers encounter. When someone is told that they 'must' stay in hospital, this is not strictly speaking a legal statement – it is an 'ought' statement, meaning it is in their interests – but it is also one to which older people, especially, would probably acquiesce. This is a classic example of passive consent. Someone is told that an action is necessary, which is not altogether what they want to do, but they do not not actively resist compliance and therefore it is assumed that they have given consent.

All of this really matters in the context of mental capacity and empowerment, for it is assumed that the person is able to give consent, either overtly and actively, or passively by compliance and not resisting. Yet this raises significant issues for social work practice.

> **PRACTICE FOCUS**
>
> What happens if someone is unable to understand what is in their own best interests? What happens, in the example of Mrs Smith above, if she is so worried about her cat that she insists on going home?

An objective observer would conclude that Mrs Smith has her priorities wrong: at this particular point in time, the cat's welfare counts far less than her own, and Mrs Smith really ought to agree to what medical staff are proposing. Is she truly able to understand her situation, is she able to evaluate the information the medical staff are setting before her, and is she appropriately evaluating that information? These surely are all pertinent questions, and they are questions now enshrined in statute law in the form of the Mental Capacity Act 2005.

The first few sections of the Mental Capacity Act 2005 clarify what happens when someone does not have full capacity to make informed decisions of this kind. In order to do this, the Act breaks down the considerations into their component parts. First of all, the legislation declares some general principles that apply in all cases. Secondly, it then attempts to clarify in what circumstances someone can be considered to have lost their capacity to make decisions themselves. Thirdly, it defines what constitutes a properly made decision using the notion of 'best interests' as a yardstick by which to determine the validity of actions taken on behalf of other people. As a consequence, the Mental Capacity Act 2005 comes close to matching the requirements and expectations of the ECHR, although there has had to be one amendment to it in order to meet Convention requirements, as will be seen in Chapter 5.

Who lacks capacity?

An adult, that is someone of the age of 16 years or above, lacks capacity if they are unable to make decisions 'because of an impairment of, or a disturbance in the functioning of, the mind or brain' which can be 'permanent or temporary' (s. 2 (1)(2) Mental Capacity Act 2005). Section 2(5) reiterates that decisions cannot be made on behalf of anyone under 16 – presumably so as to avoid a conflict with child care legislation which makes it clear that parents, or someone who has been granted parental responsibility by agreement or court order, generally decide on behalf of children under the age of consent (this was discussed more fully in Chapter 1). Capacity is not to be determined simply by reference to someone's age, appearance, condition or aspect of behaviour (s. 2(3) Mental Capacity Act 2005).

In practice what does this mean? Examples cited in the *Mental Capacity Act 2005 Code of Practice* (Department for Constitutional Affairs, 2007: para. 4.12) include:

- conditions associated with some forms of mental illness;
- dementia;
- significant learning disabilities;
- the long-term effects of brain damage;
- physical or medical conditions that cause confusion, drowsiness or loss of consciousness;
- delirium;
- concussion following a head injury;
- symptoms of alcohol or drug use.

This list is not exhaustive, with the legislation being deliberately framed so that it allows for flexibility of interpretation, but always with the understanding that, unless someone has a clearly identifiable impairment or disturbance in functioning of mind or brain, they will always have the capacity to make their own decisions. In this sense the Act is empowering of everyone who has capacity, but in relation to those who do not, it attempts to be empowering by clarifying some key principles in relation to when decisions can be made on behalf of other people.

One way in which the Act (in s. 3) does this is by itemizing the components of the decision-making process whereby the ability to make a decision is impaired if someone is unable to carry out all of the following:

- understand information relevant to the decision;
- retain the information;
- use or weigh that information as part of the process of making the decision;

- communicate that decision, which does not necessarily have to be oral communication.

To amplify this last point, s. 3(2) declares that someone is not to be regarded as lacking capacity if they can understand explanations that are 'appropriate'.

On-the-spot question	1 Consider what other means of communication social workers could use with someone who is unable to communicate verbally. 2 Could this kind of communication be considered 'appropriate'?

Both the Act and the Code of Practice (para. 4.18) suggest 'appropriate' means of communication might include simple language, sign language, visual representations, computer-mediated means of communication, visual illustrations, repeating information several times, audiotapes, video or posters. To which might be added multimedia advocacy that may be of particular benefit as it takes advantage of the opportunities offered by advances in information technology in order to extend the range of communication tools available to professionals (see SCIE (2013) reference at the end of this chapter).

The Code of Practice also suggests that retaining information is not necessarily affected if someone can only retain information for a comparatively short period (para. 4.20) and that weighing information needs to be assessed in the context. It then suggests:

> For example, a person with the eating disorder anorexia nervosa may understand information about the consequences of not eating. But their compulsion not to eat might be too strong for them to ignore. Some people who have serious brain damage might make impulsive decisions regardless of information they have been given or their understanding of it.
>
> *Department for Constitutional Affairs, 2007: para. 4.21*

Inability to communicate is quite specific and is in effect referring to people who are unconscious or in a coma. The term 'inability' certainly does not apply to someone who simply has difficulties in making themselves understood through a speech impediment, for example. The Code of Practice advocates use of speech and language therapists or specialists in non-verbal communication, if need be, to check out whether someone really is unable to communicate. This underlines the obligation already mentioned in the 'Introduction' to this book to assist people making decisions for themselves:

> A person is not to be treated as unable to make a decision unless all practicable steps to help him to do so have been taken without success. (s. 1(3) Mental Capacity Act 2005)

Chapter 3 of the Code of Practice puts forward a number of different ways of doing this. In para. 4.36 the Code reiterates the Act's presumption of capacity and then suggests that if there is doubt about someone's competence to make decisions for themselves the following questions should be asked:

- Does the person have all relevant information they need to make the decision?
- If they are making a decision that involves choosing between alternatives, do they have information on all the different options?
- Would the person have a better understanding if information was explained or presented in another way?
- Are there times of day when the person's understanding is better?
- Are there locations where they may feel more at ease?
- Can a decision be put off until the circumstances are different and the person concerned may be able to make the decision?
- Can anyone else help the person to make choices or express a view?

Not surprisingly, the issue of how exactly capacity has been assessed, and what factors are to be taken into account, has arisen in a number of cases.

In one case judges were concerned that the assessment of capacity was not entirely neutral, in that professionals made unconscious assumptions about the decision the service user ought to make (see page 65).

This summary necessarily truncates some of the circumstances and debates that featured in the case. On the surface it may appear odd that professionals appeared quite ready to override consent, but clearly they were convinced that there was a strong element of risk (and there was no doubt that the number of calls to the emergency services was excessive). The court, in its deliberations, acknowledged the dilemmas for professionals having to operate in a risk-averse culture and in that context their actions were quite understandable. Nevertheless, one of

> **KEY CASE ANALYSIS**

CC v KK and STCC [2012]

This case concerned an 82-year-old woman, KK, who had Parkinson's disease, vascular dementia and mobility problems. She had been admitted to a nursing home but did not wish to remain there. The social services department was very concerned about her frequent falls and extensive use of an emergency call service. Professionals had decided she did not have capacity to make decisions for herself and therefore were justified in invoking the Deprivation of Liberty Safeguards provisions in the Mental Capacity Act 2005 (these safeguards are explained in Chapter 5).

One of the issues for the court to consider was whether KK had capacity. The court ruled that in assessing capacity 'it was inappropriate to start with a blank canvas'. The person should be presented with detailed options so that their capacity to weigh up those options can be fairly assessed. There is a real danger, the court declared in its judgment, that professionals might 'consciously or subconsciously attach excessive weight to their own views of how her physical safety might be best protected and insufficient weight to her own views of how her emotional needs might be met'. The court also ruled that the local authority had not tried sufficiently to put together a complete package of support in anticipation of a return home, and this had effectively predetermined the assessment of capacity.

It was considered that KK might well have 'underestimated or minimised some of her needs' yet she had not 'done so to an extent that suggested that she lacked capacity to weigh up information'. Her level of understanding was not superficial. The court concluded: 'The fact that KK needed to be helped about overusing her lifeline, or reminded to eat and drink regularly, had not carried much weight in the assessment of her capacity. She had demonstrated a degree of discernment and had not simply been stating that she wanted to go home without thinking about the consequences.'

the implicit purposes of the Mental Capacity Act 2005 is to circumscribe professional power and entitle people to opt for a risky course of action if that is what they wish to do. In this case, although the wish appeared unreasonable, it did not, of itself, demonstrate that that person lacked capacity. In this sense security does not override autonomy.

In a case that has some similarities in terms of courts discouraging local authorities from adopting a totally risk averse approach to decisions,

Cardiff County Council v Ross and Davies [2011], an 82-year-old woman who had a diagnosis of dementia was allowed by the courts to go on a cruise holiday. She had previously enjoyed cruises, but was now a resident in a care home, although she spent weekends with her partner who was willing to take responsibility for her on the cruise. The local authority, declaring that she did not have capacity, had decided that it would not be in her best interests to go since there was an element of risk which she was unable to appreciate. However, the courts declared that this was insufficient to go against the presumption in favour of capacity, and implied that people's wishes should generally be respected, even if there was an element of risk. In effect the court was saying, again, that best interests does not mean safety and security override autonomy.

In *RT and LT v A Local Authority* [2010], the judge directly addressed the question of how the list in s. 3 Mental Capacity Act 2005 (see above) was to be interpreted. In this case, there was a dispute about whether a young woman, LT, should remain in residential care or return to her adoptive parents' home. She had epilepsy, learning disabilities, and a variety of diagnoses concerning extremely immature behaviour. The issue for the courts to decide was relatively straightforward in that it solely concerned whether LT, aged 23, had the capacity to decide where she should live and what contact she should have with members of her family. The judge quickly concluded that the list in s. 3 is not cumulative, but that each subsection stands in its own right, in other words if someone fails to understand information, or retain it, or evaluate it or communicate it, they are deemed not to have capacity. Here, while there was some question about whether she could understand information, expert evidence suggested clearly that she could not weigh up information as part of the decision-making process. In essence she simply said repeatedly 'I want to go home', but could not enter into a discussion about it. The expert witness referred to this as a 'wall' and on that basis the court had no difficulty concluding that she was unable to evaluate information and therefore, in accordance with the provisions of s. 3, she did not have capacity. She could not assess pros and cons in relation to contact or a question about where she was to live.

On-the-spot question

Building on this interpretation, how should social workers set about assessing capacity in circumstances where capacity is questionable or fluctuating?

These judgments offer a guide as to the way in which courts interpret the assessment requirements of the Act, and decisions in other cases have been consistent with this approach. Consequently, from a practitioner point of view, it is important to reiterate how s. 3 is central to the assessment of capacity. If there is any evidence that someone can understand, retain, evaluate and communicate a decision then the presumption is that they will be deemed to have capacity. Capacity is also act and context specific. A person is not to be treated as lacking capacity unless 'all practicable steps to help him to do so have been taken without success' (s. 1(3) Mental Capacity Act 2005). In *D Borough Council v AB* [2011], the court had to decide whether a young man should be given sex education despite a psychiatrist's objections on the grounds that it was not in his best interests. The court ruled that, notwithstanding the psychiatrist's view, sex education had to be attempted since this is what this particular section of the Act required.

All of this implies that, even if capacity is fluctuating, there may still have to be an assessment of the extent to which judgment is impaired. So, for example, if there is only occasional fleeting understanding of what is involved, would that be sufficient to say that someone truly understands? Occasional problems in relation to short-term memory would not of themselves indicate that someone had lost capacity. Yet substantive problems with memory retention that led to only very occasional, fleeting, moments of insight would be more problematic. Whether such moments could be considered decisive would depend very much on the specific situation and background of the person with memory problems. Certainly, capacity is far from easy to assess in some cases. Occasionally, expert evidence might be necessary but generally speaking assessing capacity should be well within the capabilities of experienced social work practitioners.

Empowerment and best interests

By now it should be clear that the Mental Capacity Act 2005 is strongly empowering of people who may not have full capacity to make decisions and this section outlines the key parts of the Act that underpin that empowerment. It may be helpful at this stage to outline the order in which questions need to be addressed when it comes to considering making a decision that is in someone's best interests.

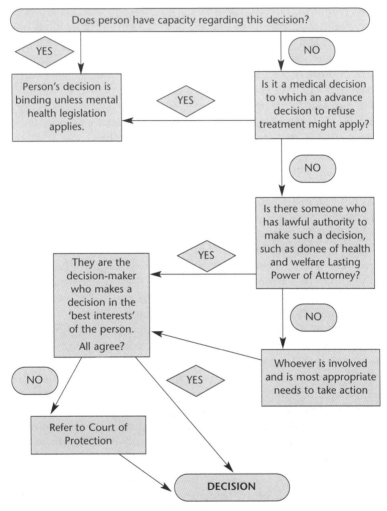

Figure 3.1: Capacity and decision-making

Section 1 Mental Capacity Act 2005 contains a series of important principles and safeguards that are both consistent with general social work principles and, more significantly from a legal perspective, are also compliant with the expectations of the ECHR regarding rights to liberty and family life (Articles 5 and 8). As outlined in the 'Introduction' to this book, s. 1 declares a presumption of capacity, making it quite explicit (in subs. (3)) that people are entitled to make unwise decisions if they have capacity. Imprudent, rash or even irresponsible decisions do not indicate a lack of capacity. The discussion then turns to subs. (5) which states:

> An act done, or decision made, under this Act for or on behalf of a person who lacks capacity must be done, or made, in his best interests (s. 1(5) Mental Capacity Act 2005)

This obligation on decision-makers, who of course need not be professionals, is amplified in s. 4 which begins by restating the requirement not to base decisions simply on someone's age, appearance, or behaviour. The decision-maker must 'consider all the relevant circumstances' and specifically must consider when someone is likely to regain capacity, and then:

> must, so far as reasonably practicable, permit and encourage the person to participate, or to improve his ability to participate, as fully as possible in any act done for him and any decision affecting him (s. 4(4) Mental Capacity Act 2005).

If the decision relates to life-sustaining treatment, the decision-maker must not 'be motivated by a desire to bring about his death' (s. 4(5) Mental Capacity Act 2005).

The *Explanatory Notes* clarify that this means:

> that whatever a decision-maker personally feels about, or wants for, the person concerned this must not affect his assessment of whether a particular treatment is in the person's best interests. This subsection does not change the previously understood common law on best interests. It does not mean that doctors are under an obligation to provide, or to continue to provide, life-sustaining treatment where that treatment is not in the best interests of the person.
>
> *HM Government, 2005: para. 31*

Consideration must also be given to:

    (a) the person's past and present wishes and feelings (and, in particular, any relevant written statement made by him when he had capacity),

    (b) the beliefs and values that would be likely to influence his decision if he had capacity, and

    (c) the other factors that he would be likely to consider if he were able to do so.

s. 4(6) Mental Capacity Act 2005

In addition, there is an obligation, insofar as it is practicable and appropriate to do so, to consult and take into account the views of:

    (a) anyone named by the person as someone to be consulted on the matter in question or on matters of that kind,

    (b) anyone engaged in caring for the person or interested in his welfare,

    (c) any donee of a lasting power of attorney granted by the person, and

    (d) any deputy appointed for the person by the court.

s. 4(7) Mental Capacity Act 2005

The *Explanatory Notes* (HM Government, 2005: para. 33) point out that such people may well have important information about the person's past wishes and feelings, beliefs and values, all of which should be taken into account. Examples of people who should be consulted include informal carers, family and friends and anyone involved in a professional or voluntary capacity, including an advocate. Without question it should include anyone appointed under a Lasting Power of Attorney (see Chapter 6 for explanation of what this is). Determining what is in someone's best interests, therefore, is an objective decision made on the basis of an independent assessment that takes into account any known views or feelings.

    Guidance as to how a best interests assessment should be undertaken is offered in the *Mental Capacity Act 2005 Code of Practice* (Department for Constitutional Affairs, 2007: ch. 5). This includes (at 65–66) a useful checklist summarizing factors to take into consideration when undertaking a best interests assessment. In brief these are:

- finding out the person's views as best as can be ascertained including:
  - their past and present wishes and feelings, however expressed
  - their beliefs and values
  - any other factors there will be likely to consider;
- at the same time do whatever is possible to encourage participation and improve their ability to take part in decision-making process;
- identify all the things that the person who lacks capacity ought to be taking into account;

- avoid discrimination of any kind including assumptions about
  - age
  - appearance
  - condition or behaviour
  - the person's quality of life;
- consider whether it is possible that the person may regain capacity (possible circumstances are listed in the Code of Practice: para. 5.28);
- wherever practicable and appropriate, consult people who may have information about the person's best interests, wishes and feelings, beliefs and values, especially:
  - someone named now or in the past by the person as someone to be consulted
  - anyone involved in caring for the person
  - close relatives or friends who have taken an interest
  - someone appointed under a Lasting Power of Attorney or **deputy** appointed by the Court of Protection (for further explanation of these terms see Chapter 6);
- where major decisions are made about medical treatment or where someone should live, in the absence of appropriate people to consult an IMCA should be appointed (IMCAs are covered in Chapter 6).

How exactly all of this is interpreted in practice will obviously depend on individual circumstances, but it may be helpful to look at an example of how the court might approach this in a case which is not just relevant to social work, but raised issues of how the Mental Capacity Act 2005 should be balanced with Article 8 ECHR concerning rights to family life (see page 72). In this case, the court had to make a decision about how the Mental Capacity Act 2005 best interests requirements related to the right to family life enshrined in Article 8 ECHR.

In this case the court effectively concluded that the Mental Capacity Act 2005 was the starting point and that Convention rights were then one factor to be taken into account, an important factor since going against Convention rights is a significant step but is acceptable if it is a 'proportionate' act, which in essence refers to the interference with the right being justified. Specifically the proportionality test includes consideration that the measure is carefully designed to meet the objective in question, that it is not arbitrary or unfair, and that the limitation impairs rights as little as possible (Hoffman, 2003:89–90).

> **KEY CASE ANALYSIS**

K v A Local Authority and Others [2012]

A judge ruled that a local authority plan to place a young adult with learning disabilities in a placement away from home for a trial period was in his best interests. This was against the father's wishes and the father appealed on the grounds that this decision violated the right to respect for family life as enshrined in the ECHR. The question the court had to address was: which comes first – the Mental Capacity Act 2005 duty to make decisions in people's best interests when they cannot make decisions for themselves, or the Convention rights?

At the first hearing the judge decided that s. 4 Mental Capacity Act 2005 had to be considered first and although she had to include in her thinking what the ECHR said about family rights, the judge decided this was not the starting point. Section 4(4) Mental Capacity Act 2005 required that all relevant circumstances would be considered, and that the person making the decision 'must, so far as reasonably practicable, permit and encourage the person to participate, or to improve his ability to participate, as fully as possible in any act done for him and any decision affecting him'.

The Appeal Court confirmed that it was correct first to ascertain the best interests of the incapacitated person by going through the s. 4 checklist. The judge then had to consider whether the results of this consideration would violate Article 8, and if they did, whether this violation was proportionate. The appeal was therefore dismissed.

Advance decisions

PRACTICE FOCUS

Laura has been warned by her general practitioner (GP) that, in addition to having a number of physical disabilities, she now has the early signs of dementia. She has already made it clear verbally to her closest friend that, in the event of her suffering any kind of serious illness which is life-threatening, she does not wish to be artificially resuscitated. Specifically, she does not want to be placed on a ventilator or to be fed artificially. Furthermore, she has specific preferences with regards to certain other forms of medical treatment and, in the event of not being able to care for herself, would prefer a small group-living arrangement rather than a large impersonal residential establishment.

However, Laura is concerned that if her dementia becomes more acute, her wishes may not be respected.

This is the kind of scenario where the Mental Capacity Act 2005 provisions for advance decisions really help. The Act gives people the right to declare some of their wishes in advance in the secure knowledge that specific requests will be acted upon, whatever their subsequent state of mind in relation to capacity. The Act does this, firstly, by clarifying what kind of decisions can be made by someone in advance. Secondly, it sets out how this decision should be declared. Thirdly, the Act stipulates how healthcare and social care professionals should respond if they are made aware of the advance decision. In relation to this last point, there are specific requirements in other legislative provision for social workers (and others) to consider any advance decision when making decisions on behalf of other people. This relates in particular to BIAs (see Chapter 5).

In the practice focus example above there are effectively two sorts of views which Laura has expressed. First of all she has stipulated that there are certain kinds of treatment she does not wish to have. Providing these stipulations comply with legal requirements, these become decisions made in advance and will be binding and, as will be seen, apply whatever the consequences. In addition she has expressed a certain number of wishes and views. These are not legally binding, but should be taken very seriously and treated as more than just preferences. Effectively, they should be complied with unless there is a strong reason for going against them. Substitute decision-makers will clearly want to look to the consequences as part of an overall assessment of what is in someone's best interests, but always bearing in mind what the person's wishes are.

The need for legislation regarding advance decisions became apparent in a number of high-profile cases in the 1980s and 1990s which had to be decided on the basis of common law and use of what is referred to as the High Court's inherent jurisdiction. The most well-known of these is probably the case of Tony Bland who was in hospital on a life-support machine as a result of injuries sustained in the Hillsborough football disaster in 1989. Medical opinion declared no real possibility of recovery and relatives wanted his life to be ended, but clinicians did not consider they had the legal authority to do this. Having considered all the circumstances, the courts gave them that authority (*Airedale NHS Trust v Bland* [1993]).

More challenging for the courts, in the sense that an articulate person argued forcefully that she should not be compelled to stay alive, was the case of Ms B.

> **KEY CASE ANALYSIS**

Ms B v An NHS Hospital Trust [2002]

In February 2001 Ms B, who had become completely paralysed from the neck down, was placed on a ventilator. Her requests for it to be withdrawn were overridden by doctors who considered that she was not competent to make that decision. There were different psychiatric opinions about whether she had capacity but eventually they concluded that she did. Nevertheless, doctors continued to refuse to withdraw treatment. Ms B also refused to go to a spinal unit or to a hospice, since both medical establishments were unlikely to agree to her request for her life to end by the withdrawal of what was, in effect, an artificial means of keeping her alive.

Ms B asked the High Court for a declaration that she was competent to refuse life-prolonging medical treatment.

The judge decided that the crucial issue was whether Ms B was able to comprehend the information concerning her decision, whether she was able to use the information and weigh it in the balance as part of the process of arriving at a decision, and most especially whether she understood the implications and consequences of refusing treatment.

The judge decided that Ms B was indeed competent, reiterating the legal presumption that adults possess mental capacity. The judge was entirely satisfied that Ms B was competent to make all relevant decisions about her medical treatment, including the decision to refuse ventilation. She could therefore make that decision, even though it would in effect end her life.

This judgment was made before the passing of the Mental Capacity Act 2005, and indeed some of the influences of the judgment (which was made by the President of the Family Division of the High Court) can be discerned in the Act itself, particularly the factors that constitute capacity to make a valid decision. It is worth noting in passing, and it is an important safeguard, that decisions relating to treatments that may affect someone's life can only be made in relation to withdrawal of treatment or refusing to undergo specific forms of treatment. Under no circumstances can an advance decision authorize medical professionals to take active action that would directly end someone's life; they can only withdraw treatment, or not offer treatment, that might otherwise keep someone alive. This may seem a very fine line, but it is essentially the difference between assisted suicide, which emphatically the law does not permit in the UK since it is potentially manslaughter (see further reading at end of this chapter), and decisions to refuse certain kinds of treatment, which the law does now permit within very precise parameters.

On-the-spot questions   1 What are these parameters?
2 How might they apply in Laura's case?

Essentially the parameters are that someone has full capacity to understand the potentially fatal consequences of refusing treatment, or else that there is an advance decision made that specifies the circumstances in which treatment is to be refused, given that this cannot apply to treatments that can lawfully be imposed against someone's wishes, for example, under Part IV Mental Health Act 1983. The minimum age for making an advance decision is 18 (s. 24(1) Mental Capacity Act 2005). Obviously, the person has to have capacity to make the advance decision, but bear in mind that they may have capacity in relation to some matters and not others, as s. 3 of the Act implies. The kind of decision that can be made is limited, being confined to treatment that 'is proposed to be carried out or continued by a person providing healthcare' (s. 24 (1)(a)). Note that it does not relate to social care, so it is not possible to use advance decisions in order to secure a place in a particular residential establishment, for example, or to insist on certain kinds of resources to provide community care.

So, in our Practice Focus example, Laura could not actually make an advance decision about small-group care as opposed to a large residential home. Nor can advance decisions be used to insist on certain kinds of medical treatment. The purpose of an advance decision is to ensure that a decision to refuse medical treatment is one that will be acted upon even if the person loses capacity to give or refuse consent at the time the treatment is needed. It gives healthcare professionals protection from liability if they stop or withhold treatment on the basis of what the advance decision says. If an advance decision concerns life-sustaining treatment it must be made in writing and signed and witnessed, with a statement included that this decision applies even if the person's life is at risk. Since the advance decision can be withdrawn or varied at any time, it is incumbent upon healthcare professionals to find out if there have been any changes in the person's view since the advance decision was made.

Whilst it is acceptable for advance decisions to set out in lay terms what kinds of treatment someone is refusing, there is always the possibility that this list may not be comprehensive, so one alternative might be to nominate in advance someone who would take a more general responsibility for making decisions on behalf of someone else. This arrangement would be a Lasting Power of Attorney and this is discussed in more detail in Chapter 6.

Advance decisions do not override statute law, however, so it is not possible to order people to act in such a way that would help them commit suicide, nor does it necessarily prevent treatment being given to people compulsorily detained under the Mental Health Act 1983 (see next chapter).

So can Laura, in our case study, make an advance decision that she does not want artificial resuscitation? The short answer is yes she can, providing at this moment she has the capacity to make that decision. Given that she has a diagnosis of dementia, in order to ensure that her wishes are complied with, it would be prudent to do more than the legal minimum, that is more than just having her wishes written down and witnessed. She might be best advised to have independent, professional confirmation that she has capacity to make the advance decision. It would be important to ensure that this decision was recorded in her healthcare records and elsewhere, so that people knew what her wishes were. Unless healthcare professionals are aware of the existence of an advance decision, they are obliged to act in what they deem to be perceived as someone's best interests, which may not accord with what Laura wants. It would certainly be advisable to ensure that as many people as possible are aware of the existence of the advance decision, so that no one is in any doubt as to what her wishes are for future care.

In cases where there is uncertainty about whether an advance decision exists, or what it actually means, it is possible to ask for a decision from the Court of Protection, although the court does not have the power to overturn a valid advance decision. It can adjudicate on whether someone has capacity to make an advance decision and whether it should apply in particular circumstances (ss 16 and 17 Mental Capacity Act 2005). The role of the Court of Protection is discussed more generally in Chapter 6.

Conclusion

This chapter explored some of the fundamental principles that relate to mental capacity legislation. It included a discussion of what is meant by consent and how capacity is to be assessed, which included references to case law examples that demonstrate how courts make judgments about capacity. The significance of the term 'best interests' was highlighted and explained, with further references to official guidance and case law. The chapter concluded with an explanation of advance decisions, with indications of their benefits and limitations. The next chapter considers the interconnections between mental capacity and mental health legislation, an area of particular concern for many social work practitioners in adult care since there is obviously a desire to empower people who have mental health problems, yet concern that they may not always make decisions that are in their own best interests.

Further reading

Department for Constitutional Affairs (2007) *Mental Capacity Act 2005 Code of Practice.* This is invaluable in setting out the principles, provisions and requirements of the Mental Capacity Act 2005 in relation to practice. It has separate chapters devoted to several topics covered in this book. Most relevant to the topics covered in this chapter are chapter 2 (on the statutory principles), chapter 4 (on assessment of capacity), chapter 5 (on best interests) and chapter 9 (on advance decisions).

Director of Public Prosecutions (2010) *Policy for Prosecutors in Cases of Encouraging or Assisting Suicide* is an important document for practitioners involved in end-of-life cases. Following the *Purdy* case (*R (on the Application of Purdy) v DPP* [2009]) in which courts refused Debbie Purdy any assurance in advance that her husband would not be prosecuted for helping her to die, the House of Lords ordered the Director of Public Prosecutions (DPP) to issue guidance available to the public on what the law said about assisted suicide and how the DPP would interpret it.

McDonald, A (2010) 'The impact of the 2005 Mental Capacity Act on social workers' decision making and approaches to the assessment of risk' 40 *British Journal of Social Work* 1229–46 reports on research into the impact of the Mental Capacity Act 2005 on social work practice concerning analysis of risk with older people. It identifies three approaches to risk: legalistic, actuarial and rights-based and argues in favour of rights-based approach.

Social Care Institute for Excellence (2011) *Mental Capacity Act (MCA) Resource* is a useful overview of the Mental Capacity Act 2005 that includes e-learning materials. These aim to be no more than an introduction, but do focus on specific aspects of practice in relation to the Mental Capacity Act 2005: helping people to make their decisions and making best interests decisions on other people's behalf in particular.

Social Care Institute for Excellence (2013) *Get Connected* is a project that enables 'providers of care for adults in England to access information and communication technology more effectively'.

4

MENTAL HEALTH, MENTAL CAPACITY AND EMPOWERMENT

To what extent can people with serious mental health problems make decisions for themselves? What does the law say regarding the account-ability of people with enduring mental health problems for their own decisions? To what extent can people who have serious mental health issues make decisions in relation to their treatment, especially when that treatment may not relate to mental health matters? How does the law that provides for compulsory admission to hospital in the most serious cases connect to the Mental Capacity Act 2005 with its presumption of capacity and empowerment principles? Where exactly is the boundary between compulsory powers in mental health law and the measures that can override people's absolute rights to autonomous decision-making in the Mental Capacity Act 2005?

These are all very real questions for practitioners in the mental health field. Whilst accepting the principles underpinning the Mental Capacity Act 2005, especially in relation to encouraging people to make their own decisions to the fullest extent that they are able, there may still be a resid-ual concern that people are not able to make decisions in their own best interests because of a mental disorder. These are also questions that have occurred in a number of landmark case law decisions, which have drawn a sharp distinction between treatment decisions relating to mental 'disorder' and all other kinds of decisions. There is also now clear guid-ance from the courts concerning the relationship between mental health and mental capacity legislation.

The relationship between mental health and mental capacity legislation

Definitions

Generally speaking, mental health and mental capacity are distinct, or as one legal text puts it 'mental disorder and mental incapacity are differ-ent concepts' (Bartlett, 2008: para. 5.38). However, there is one impor-tant area in which the Mental Capacity Act 2005 relies on definitions in the Mental Health Act 1983. Chapter 2 outlined the specific measures that were introduced to address the 'Bournewood gap' by amending s. 4 Mental Capacity Act 2005, such amendments usually being referred to as the Deprivation of Liberty Safeguards (the main topic for the next chapter). These amendments apply only to people who have a 'mental disorder', as now defined in s. 1 Mental Health Act 1983 which declares '"mental disorder" means any disorder or disability of the mind' (s. 1(2), but includes the following riders:

(3) Dependence on alcohol or drugs is not considered to be a disorder or disability of the mind ...
(4) 'learning disability' means a state of arrested or incomplete development of the mind which includes significant impairment of intelligence and social functioning ...

s. 1 Mental Health Act 1983

There is a further proviso that restricts the use of compulsory powers for people with learning disabilities, but this does not apply to the definition of disorder relevant to Deprivation of Liberty Safeguards. The *Mental Health Act Code of Practice* (Department of Health, 2008: para. 3.3) sets out a list of conditions which are generally recognized as forms of mental disorder. The list is much wider than forms of psychotic conditions (although these are listed) and includes the following:

• organic mental disorder such as dementia and delirium;
• personality and behavioural changes caused by brain injury or damage;
• personality disorders;
• eating disorders;
• autistic spectrum disorders including Asperger's syndrome.

When it comes to deprivation of liberty, the starting point for both sets of legislation, mental health and mental capacity, therefore, is whether someone has a mental disorder. If they do not, they cannot lose the right to autonomy in terms of choosing where they live (save, very exceptionally, if they qualify for removal under s. 47 National Assistance Act 1948, which is very rare and is in effect a public health order – see discussion elsewhere in this book and Brammer, 2013:520–21).

Empowerment

Taking a broad view of mental capacity legislation and court decisions regarding capacity, it would be fair to say that the general approach is benign. The concern is to protect and empower: to protect people from themselves where they are unable to make decisions or risk being exploited by others (see Chapter 6 for further discussion on this) at the same time as insisting that professionals act in the best interests of the person, encouraging them to take as wide a range of decisions as they can for themselves (ss 1(5) and 4(4) Mental Capacity Act 2005). Mental health legislation appears to have a different orientation, as can be seen very clearly by the way the legislation is formulated. Whereas the Mental Capacity Act 2005 begins with a whole set of principles concerning definitions and clarification of capacity as a legal concept, the Mental Health Act 1983 moves immediately from a definition of mental disorder (s. 1 as amended by the Mental Health Act 2007) into grounds for detention in hospital (ss 2, 3, 4, 5 and 37 Mental Health Act 1983). There is no definition of mental health in mental health legislation, nor indeed any principles concerning empowerment included. Consequently, it would appear that mental health legislation is not so much about empowering service users as protecting them from themselves, or protecting other people from them. It does this by authorizing specific professionals to apply for them to be compulsorily admitted to hospital and detained there.

Grounds for intervention

The limited circumstances in which people can be deprived of their liberty, either in a registered care home or hospital, under mental capacity legislation relate solely to their personal needs and assessment of their best interests (fuller explanation in next chapter). Grounds for detention under the Mental Health Act 1983, which invariably means admission to hospital, relate not just to the 'interests' of the person's 'own health or safety' but also 'with a view to the protection of others' (s. 2(2) Mental Health Act 1983). Admission to psychiatric hospital must be for the purpose of treatment and, for longer-term orders, it is a requirement that 'appropriate medical treatment is available' (s. 3 Mental Health Act 1983 as amended). It is not the purpose here to explore how these criteria are to be applied generally but to note key differences as regards capacity and empowerment issues, which in turn means exploring the different circumstances in which mental health and mental capacity laws may apply. For full consideration of the law relating to compulsory admission and detention in hospital under the Mental Health Act 1983 (as amended by the Mental Health Act 2007) reference should be made to one of the standard social work law or mental health specific texts (Barber et al., 2012; Jones, 2012; Brammer, 2013; Brayne and Carr, 2013).

Age

One threshold difference between the two sets of legislation is the minimum age at which the respective laws apply. There are no age limits in the Mental Health Act 1983, so potentially the Act can apply to anyone including children and young people, although whether it should is another matter since it raises significant ethical issues.

Indeed, there are now plenty of examples of young people being subject to the compulsory detention powers in mental health legislation, although obviously they are also subject to the provisions in statutory and common law-related child care legislation, including the jurisdiction of their parents if they are not yet *Gillick* competent (see Chapter 1). The Mental Capacity Act 2005 has a general threshold age of 16, although in relation to Deprivation of Liberty Safeguards this minimum age is 18. Under-18s come under the jurisdiction of parental powers, the local authority acting under the Children Act 1989, or the High Court using its wardship or inherent jurisdiction authority (subject to s. 100 Children Act 1989).

Professional decision-makers

The Mental Health Act 2007 stipulates that applications for compulsory admissions to hospital may be made by Approved Mental Health Professionals, approved in this context meaning having undertaken specific forms of training (s. 18). The role is restricted to certain groups: social workers, certain categories of nurses, occupational therapists and chartered psychologists (Mental Health (Approval of Persons to be Approved Mental Health Professionals) (England) Regulations 2008; Mental Health (Approval of Persons to be Approved Mental Health Professionals) (Wales) Regulations 2008). They have certain designated tasks connected to the admission process and in relation to patients discharged from hospital under community treatment orders (Brown et al., 2012; Brown, 2013). Applications are based on medical recommendations made by doctors who meet certain specified requirements (s. 12 Mental Health Act 1983).

The Mental Capacity Act 2005 in relation to deprivation of liberty operates rather differently, in that the key decision-maker is the BIA who can be a social worker, nurse, occupational therapist or psychologist who has undergone the specified training, categories distinct from those applicable to Approved Mental Health Professionals, although there is nothing to stop someone undertaking both sets of training, having dual approval, and playing both roles. Recommendations to the **Supervisory Body** are the sole prerogative of the BIA taking into account their own assessments and those conducted by other professionals (see the next chapter for a full explanation of this process). The role relates solely to a decision as to whether to recommend that someone be compelled to remain in a specified care home or hospital.

Treatment

There is no automatic restriction of people's rights to accept or refuse treatment simply because they are detained patients under the Mental Health Act 1983. An informal patient, that is someone who has given, or is assumed to have given, consent to being in a psychiatric hospital is in the same position as someone who is in a general hospital and the provisions of the Mental Capacity Act 2005 in relation to treatment in people's best interests apply. That means to say that treatment either has to be with active consent or else compliant with common law and the requirements of s. 5 Mental Capacity Act 2005:

> An act done, or decision made under this Act for or on behalf of a
> person who lacks capacity must be done, or made, in his best interests.

Such actions cannot override advance decisions. They could include taking action when someone is unconscious, or action necessary to keep someone alive, to which special provisions apply (see s. 4(5) Mental Capacity Act 2005). There is useful guidance with case examples on the application of the best interests principle in the *Mental Capacity Act Code of Practice* (Department for Constitutional Affairs, 2007: ch. 5).

The difference for patients detained under sections of the Mental Health Act 1983 is that they can be compelled to accept treatment whilst in hospital under Part IV of the Act. Section 63 allows for most kinds of treatment to be given for the first three months without consent if necessary, but this is subject to ECHR requirements and ought to comply with guidance contained in *The Mental Health Act Code of Practice* (Department of Health, 2008). The Mental Capacity Act 2005 does not override mental health legislation in this regard. It may be worth noting that special provision now applies to electro-convulsive therapy (s. 58A Mental Health Act 1983) which cannot be given if it conflicts with an advance decision, a decision by someone holding Lasting Power of Attorney, or directions from the Court of Protection (see Chapter 6 for further discussion of Lasting Power of Attorney and the Court of Protection). A patient who was detained under s. 3 and is now in the community under a community treatment order (s. 17A Mental Health Act 1983) can only be compelled to accept treatment through re-admission under s. 17.

Outside hospital the Mental Capacity Act 2005 provisions apply to them in the same way as they do to everyone else.

People living in the community

There is provision in s. 7 of the Mental Health Act 1983 for guardianship, which is effectively a form of community supervision, with requirements for people to reside at a specific place (but no powers to detain or compel people to remain there), to attend places for the purpose of medical treatment, occupation, education or training, and to be visited by professionals (s. 8 Mental Health Act 1983). Provisions in the Mental Capacity Act 2005 for Lasting Power of Attorney and Court of Protection involvement may mean in some cases that people acting under the authority of the Mental Capacity Act 2005 have wider powers, including the power to convey people, which the guardianship provision essentially lacks (Barrett, 2008: para. 5.58).

Appeals

Someone detained in hospital under the Mental Health Act 1983 has the right to appeal to the hospital managers and to the mental health review tribunal, a first-level tribunal of the Health Education and Social Care Chamber. There are specific expectations of social workers involved in this process (Barber et al., 2012: ch. 12). Someone compelled to remain in a care home or hospital under the Deprivation of Liberty Safeguards can appeal to the Court of Protection, or else apply for judicial review. There is no specified role for social workers in this process.

Accountability of people with mental disorders

In the previous chapter, there was considerable emphasis on the principles underpinning the Mental Capacity Act 2005 which promote the idea of people being empowered to make decisions for themselves to the full extent that they are able. Now comes the corollary of this – namely that people are fully responsible and accountable for their actions unless there is evidence to the contrary, an important principle underpinning common law. The Mental Capacity Act 2005 reaffirms a presumption of capacity (as was explained in the 'Introduction' to this book). Common law, both criminal and civil, includes a presumption of full accountability for actions (for adults). This implies that someone has a 'sound mind'. Where they do not, yet are found guilty of a crime

> **PRACTICE FOCUS**
>
> Michael, aged 35, is diagnosed as having a bipolar affective disorder and has had a number of hospital admissions, including periods as a detained patient. However, he is currently living in the community and there are no legal orders in force. He lives with a partner who works full-time, and they have just about enough money to afford a reasonable standard of living. He recently experienced a hypomanic phase during which he spent over £3000 on items which the couple could ill afford. This might be regarded simply as a reckless spending spree, but it was self-evidently connected to his state of mental health. However, the credit card company is now actively pursuing him for debt, so Michael is arguing that he bought the goods when he was in an elated phase. The credit card company insists he has to pay the full amount, plus interest, and that if he cannot pay his partner must do so as it is a joint account.
>
> - Is Michael legally responsible for this debt?
> - Is his partner?

by a court, there are provisions for substituting detention in hospital for another kind of sentence for a criminal offence.

When it comes to incurring debt, which is a civil law matter, the presumption of capacity must necessarily mean that people are liable for their debts even though they might have temporarily lost a complete understanding of what they were doing. In this particular case, while it might not have been very sensible for Michael to have a credit card, and his partner may well rue the decision to make this a joint account, once the decision is made to allow him a card he is fully responsible for its use, unless it can be shown that the organization that supplied the card ought reasonably to have known about his condition. Otherwise, even if he were going through an acute manic phase and engaging in all sorts of reckless actions, he is still responsible for the consequences of those actions in terms of incurring the debt. This may sound particularly harsh but it is a necessary corollary of the principle that people have rights to manage their own affairs up until the point when it can be demonstrated that they are no longer capable of doing so. In this case, legal advice would be necessary since it cannot just be assumed that he is not responsible even though he has experienced spells of compulsory detention in hospital.

There are a number of strategies that might be adopted to address this, for example, having a much lower credit limit on the card, or working with Michael to determine whether having a credit card is really in his interests; but it may be that steps do have to be taken to repay the debts. Better still, naturally, would be to prevent this situation occurring in the first place, and in particular some discussion with the partner may be advisable. For the partner's position is potentially precarious, since whilst it may depend on exactly what the contract with the credit card company says, in most cases the partner will be responsible for all of the debts if they agreed to share the account: marriage or civil partnership is not a prerequisite for the partner being liable. It would not matter from the credit card company's point of view who incurred the debt; it is the account that is in debt not individual people.

The point of choosing this example is to highlight the extent of the relevant legal presumptions, which demarcate some kind of autonomy boundary. People have rights to make decisions and choices, but in order to effect those rights, they may also have responsibilities for dealing with the consequences of making wrong or ill-advised decisions. This may sound self-evident, but there can obviously be enormous personal repercussions in individual cases.

In order to demarcate the legal boundaries of autonomy, the next section of this chapter explores the extent to which people can make their own decisions regarding medical treatment, since this is the issue that has predominated in various important legal cases in the last 20 years or so, and is of direct relevance to social workers who work in medical settings or who are called upon to act as advocates.

Capacity and treatment refusals

To what extent can someone with a mental health history be allowed to make their own decision concerning medical treatment unconnected to mental health? Logically, if all adults can make decisions about agreeing and refusing treatment, that principle ought to apply regardless of all circumstances bar one, namely that the refusal to accept medical treatment is directly related to the mental disorder itself. In other words if an acute mental 'disorder' is impeding someone's ability to understand and evaluate decisions, then that might be the one circumstance where the court might overrule the decision they make.

This was what the court considered in a case that preceded the Mental Capacity Act 2005, *Re C (Adult: Refusal of Medical Treatment)* [1994]. The case concerned a man aged 68, with a diagnosis of paranoid schizophrenia, who was in Broadmoor serving a sentence imposed by the courts. He was admitted to a general hospital where a consultant considered he needed to have a gangrenous leg amputated below the knee and, unless this procedure were carried out, he had only a 15 per cent chance of survival. The patient refused, declaring that he would prefer to die with two feet rather than one. The hospital considered that he did not have capacity to make that decision, but advocates acting on his behalf argued that he did.

The judge declared that C was entitled to refuse treatment even if the probable result would be death. The question the judge asked himself was not whether the refusal was reasonable but whether the capacity of the patient had been so reduced by his long-standing mental disorder that he did not sufficiently understand the nature, purpose and effects of the medical treatment which he had been advised to accept. Although C's general capacity was considered to have been impaired by schizophrenia, he still appeared to understand the nature, purpose and effects of the treatment he was refusing. He had obviously arrived at a clear choice and this was one he was entitled to make.

This appears to be the first example of UK courts accepting the right of an adult, with a mental health history, to refuse treatment. In this particular case, it was decided that whether C was entitled to refuse treatment depended on whether ultimately he was able to understand and retain the necessary information and balance it with other considerations – a test which was carried forward, as already noted, to the Mental Capacity Act 2005.

In two cases concerning pregnancy and women with serious mental health conditions – *Tameside and Glossop Acute Services Trust v CH (A Patient)* [1996] and *Re MB* [1997] – courts overruled refusals to accept treatment where mental disorder-related beliefs were held to be distorted perceptions to the extent that these directly impinged on the ability to make decisions. However, in the following key case, using the compulsory detention powers under the Mental Health Act 1983 in order to compel someone with mental health issues to accept treatment relating to pregnancy was deemed unlawful.

> KEY CASE ANALYSIS

St George's Healthcare NHS Trust v S [1998]

A pregnant woman, S, had refused antenatal care but was persuaded by her social worker to register with the GP who diagnosed pre-eclampsia. The GP gave S advice which she refused to follow, despite being warned that failure to do so would lead possibly to her own death and/or the child's death. She declared that she wanted her baby born 'naturally'. The social worker and two doctors then decided that S should be admitted to a psychiatric hospital under s. 2 Mental Health Act 1983. Subsequently she gave birth by Caesarean section. At first she would not accept the child but later bonded with her. The s. 2 detention came to an end and she discharged herself from hospital against medical advice. Whilst in psychiatric hospital no specific treatment for any kind of mental disorder had been prescribed.

The Court of Appeal declared this inappropriate and issued more general guidance.

The Court of Appeal began with the principle that adults with capacity are entitled to make whatever decision they want, but accepted that there are occasions when someone appears to have lost capacity and therefore professionals must act in their best interests. However, the Mental Health Act 1983 'could not be deployed to achieve the detention of an individual against her will merely because her thinking process is unusual. Even when used by well-intentioned individuals for what they believe to be genuine and powerful reasons, perhaps shared by a large section of the community, unless the case falls within the prescribed conditions the Act cannot be used to justify detention.' (at 161)

In this case the grounds for s. 2 admission to a psychiatric hospital had not been fulfilled. In effect the social worker and doctors tried to use the mental health legislation in order to compel someone to accept treatment unrelated to their psychiatric condition. Therefore both treatment and admission to hospital under the Mental Health Act 1983 were unlawful.

The judgment in this case makes it absolutely plain that admission to a psychiatric hospital under the Mental Health Act 1983 is for the purpose of assessment and treatment in relation to a mental disorder. It is not for the purpose of securing other kinds of treatment, no matter how well-intentioned the professionals might be and however convinced they may be that the service user is making a decision that is not in their own best interests. It is simply using legislation designed for one purpose for something quite different. Furthermore, in order to prevent the recurrence of similar cases, the court issued guidelines which included the following (sections are omitted as the guidelines are quite long and much of it is procedural):

(i) In principle, a patient may remain competent notwithstanding detention under the Mental Health Act 1983 ...

(iii) If the patient is incapable of giving or refusing consent, either in the long term or temporarily (e.g. due to unconsciousness), the patient must be cared for according to the [health] authority's judgement of the patient's best interests. Where the patient has given an advance directive, before becoming incapable, treatment and care should normally be subject to the advance directive. However if there is reason to doubt the reliability of the advance directive (e.g. it may sensibly be thought not to apply to the circumstances which have arisen), then an application for a declaration may be made ...

Judgment in St George's Healthcare NHS Trust v S *[1998] 194–95*

The point made in this judgment about advance directives, which became known as advance decisions in the Mental Capacity Act 2005 (see Chapter 3), was tested in a case concerning an adult with severe anorexia.

The case on page 91 illustrates that courts will consider the circumstances in which someone made an advance decision and will be reluctant to authorize the implementation of an advance decision that may lead to someone's death if there is any doubt about their capacity to make the decision in the first place. Consequently it may be advisable in some cases to have confirmation that someone does have capacity to make decisions if they are considering formulating an advance decision that might relate to life-sustaining treatment.

On-the-spot question How might this principle apply in other kinds of mental health cases?

One obvious example would be where someone suffered from severe depression and tried to insist that hospital staff should not treat them if

> **KEY CASE ANALYSIS**

A Local Authority v E (by her Litigation Friend, the Official Solicitor) and Others [2012]

As well as having anorexia, E was diagnosed as having a personality disorder and was alcohol and opiate dependent. She also suffered long-term malnutrition, was considered difficult to treat, and therefore unsurprisingly had been subject to a number of periods of compulsory detention and treatment under the Mental Health Act 1983. She had made an advance decision about her medical treatment in that she declared a wish not to be force-fed and it is the validity of this that was challenged in court. For in 2012, she was detained in hospital under s. 3 Mental Health Act 1983 and fed by tube but insisted that it be stopped. Consequently it was considered likely her life would come to an end, so the question was whether she had the right to make this kind of advance decision given that its implementation was life-threatening. Whilst ordinarily the answer to this would be clear that she did, in this specific case the court had to consider whether E had the capacity to make that advance decision.

The court decided that E would not be able to make a valid advance decision if, at the time she made it, there was an impairment or disturbance in the functioning of the mind or brain. In her case this disturbance took the form of anorexia. There was no doubt that she could understand and retain information relevant to her treatment decision and could communicate it, but her obsession with weight meant that she was unable to evaluate the advantages and disadvantages of particular courses of action. The obsession with weight distorted her ability to evaluate and reason, and therefore she did not have the capacity to make the decision about force-feeding. Furthermore, if it was necessary to feed her by force this would be proportionate and therefore would not in any way interfere with her rights under the ECHR.

they attempted suicide. If this were tested, the courts would be concerned with two issues: firstly whether the person had full capacity to make that kind of advance decision when suffering from severe mental health problems, and secondly whether it would be valid to try and prevent medical staff carrying out procedures which were immediately and obviously necessary to preserve someone's life, since this is both a professional and common law obligation.

Clarifying the boundaries

> **PRACTICE FOCUS**
>
> Alan, aged 60, has a psychotic illness the origins of which partly lie in excessive drinking over a lengthy period of time. He has associated memory problems and has been treated in psychiatric hospitals at various times in the past. After having a fall and spending a week in a general hospital he was admitted to a residential home being quite incapable of looking after himself and showing no understanding of the health and safety problems created by excessive use of alcohol. Initially he settled well at the care home but has recently been visiting the local pub frequently, returning to the care home in an intoxicated state and threatening other residents and staff. The care staff believe that they must control his behaviour and debate whether to arrange a Mental Health Act 1983 admission or whether to apply restrictions under the Mental Capacity Act 2005.
>
> - Can they?
> - Should they simply choose between mental capacity and mental health legislation?
> - What should they do?

Cases such as this raise a number of practice and legal issues for practitioners. Practice issues tend to revolve around the feasibility of applying restrictions, how these fit with the care plan, and how to balance autonomy and safeguarding issues. There are also considerations regarding Alan's family, if they are involved, and the appropriateness of the placement given his age and specific needs. From a health point of view, one would want to know more about the interconnections between the psychotic illness and his alcohol-related issues, which is where this case becomes more challenging from a legal perspective (and note, as highlighted earlier in the chapter, s. 1 Mental Health Act 1983 does not allow a dependence on alcohol *on its own* to constitute a mental disorder). For, if his needs do indeed relate primarily to mental health to the extent that he needs psychiatric treatment, and he poses a risk either to himself or to other people (or to both), then the question arises why he is not being admitted to hospital under the Mental Health Act 1983. Indeed, the requirements of the Deprivation of Liberty Safeguards include an eligibility criterion which states that someone cannot be made subject to

Deprivation of Liberty Safeguards if they qualify for admission and detention in hospital under mental health legislation. But which comes first – mental health admission or the Deprivation of Liberty Safeguards?

The answer to this question is now clear, thanks to some case law decisions.

> **KEY CASE ANALYSIS**

J v The Foundation Trust and Others [2009]

J had an alcohol-related dementia and diabetes and was considered at serious risk because of self-neglect and identifiable deterioration in his mental and physical health. Following two hypoglycaemic incidents, caused by neglecting to administer his insulin injections, he was admitted to hospital under s. 2 Mental Health Act 1983, subsequently being detained under s. 3. Once he no longer needed treatment, he moved to a residential care home, but this arrangement broke down. Subsequently, he was readmitted to hospital but, instead of being detained under a Mental Health Act 1983 order, he was made subject to a standard authorization under the revised s. 4 Mental Capacity Act 2005 (see next chapter for full explanation of this legislation and standard authorizations).

J appealed to the court against this authorization, claiming that it was illegal since it failed to meet the 'eligibility' condition that prevents mental capacity legislation being used where someone qualifies for detention under mental health legislation. Thus, he regarded himself as a mental health patient and therefore, if he was to be detained, it should have been done under mental health law rather than the Mental Capacity Act 2005. The court therefore had to consider which legislation had primacy: mental health or mental capacity.

This was actually the first case to be determined since the amendments to the Mental Capacity Act 2005 were introduced by the Mental Health Act 2007 and the courts had no hesitation in saying that, if mental health legislation were applicable, then it had primacy. Specifically, the court said that decision-makers should start with the question concerning eligibility for detention under the Mental Health Act 1983; they could not 'pick and choose between the two statutory regimes as they thought fit'. However, once they had discounted the appropriateness of a compulsory mental health admission, they could consider whether J qualified for deprivation of liberty under the Mental Capacity Act 2005, bearing in mind that the criteria for that deprivation were different from those pertaining to the Mental Health Act 1983.

The court offered further guidance. Professionals should decide whether the person needs treatment for their psychiatric condition or whether the purpose of admission was to address physical treatment needs. If, in effect, the purpose was primarily to address physical health, then the mental health route would not be feasible. Since in this case treatment for diabetes was unlikely to affect his mental disorder, and was not really related to it, this of itself meant that mental health admission could not be considered and therefore the eligibility condition in the Deprivation of Liberty Safeguards was satisfied. So it was possible to authorize deprivation of liberty under the Mental Capacity Act 2005 in these circumstances.

A similar legal issue arose in *W Primary Care Trust v TB and Others* [2009] where the court had to decide whether the Mental Capacity Act 2005 provisions applied where someone appeared to be in a residential home for the purpose of receiving treatment for mental health problems. TB had a brain injury and received psychiatric treatment for her condition both in hospital and in the community. Because of the complexity of her needs, the Community Mental Health Team decided that these could not be adequately addressed by conventional drug treatments, but that her fixed delusional beliefs might be better addressed in a therapeutic residential unit. They successfully found a unit prepared to treat her but, as she would not agree to go there, the question arose as to whether she could be detained there under mental health legislation, or alternatively be kept there under the Deprivation of Liberty Safeguards of the Mental Capacity Act 2005. Mental health legislation makes it clear that compulsory detention has to be in hospital or certain kinds of nursing homes, which did not include this residential placement so mental health legislation could not be used here. The question then was: could the Mental Capacity Act 2005 be used since the purpose was to address underlying mental health problems? The court could not see a fundamental objection to this, but pointed out that this decision would centre on what was in TB's best interests.

What about the reverse scenario? Can the Mental Capacity Act 2005 be used as an alternative to compulsory powers in the Mental Health Act 1983? That is the issue raised in *R (on the Application of Sessay) v South London and Maudsley NHS Foundation Trust and Another* [2011] where someone was admitted to, and 'detained' in, a psychiatric hospital under s. 5 Mental Capacity Act 2005. In this case police were called to a woman's home where they were so concerned about her mental health that they took her to hospital for assessment. As she was not in a place to which the public has access, s. 136 Mental Health Act 1983, which gives the police limited powers to remove apparently mentally disordered people in need of care or control to a place of safety, could not be used. As this was an emergency which involved a child, who was the main focus of police attention, they were not in possession of a warrant issued by magistrates (under s. 135 Mental Health Act 1983). The police therefore argued that they could use s. 5 Mental Capacity Act 2005 in order to say that it was in her best interests to be admitted to hospital, and the hospital used the same legal grounds to cover the lengthy period that elapsed between admission to hospital and the assessments by an Approved Mental Health Professional and two doctors that eventually led to a decision to detain her under s. 2 Mental Health Act 1983.

The courts declared categorically that the police officers' use of s. 5 Mental Capacity Act 2005 was unlawful. The only police powers relating to mental health are ss 135 and 136 Mental Health Act 1983. The unlawful removal breached Articles 5 and 8 ECHR. Nor could the common law doctrine of necessity be used to justify keeping patients in hospital since the Mental Health Act 1983 has extensive provisions for assessment, admission and detention, specifically ss 2–6. In an emergency there is provision in s. 4, and if the legislation is used correctly there would be no possibility of breaching Article 5 ECHR so long as there is no undue delay.

The implication of this case is crystal clear: the Mental Capacity Act 2005 cannot be used instead of compulsory powers in the Mental Health Act 1983. If someone is in their own home and needs urgent admission to hospital, then the provisions in s. 4 of the 1983 Act come into play and the 'best interests' provisions under mental capacity legislation cannot apply.

The overriding message from these and similar cases that have been considered by the courts is that mental health legislation trumps everything else. Whether someone needs compulsory admission to a psychiatric hospital is the first consideration, and if they do then that is what must happen. If they do not, then use of mental capacity legislation can be considered, but not as a substitute for admission to a psychiatric hospital and providing, naturally, that all other criteria are met. There is nothing in principle to prevent someone being kept against their wishes in a residential care home for the purpose of treatment which could relate to their mental disorder, again so long as all the requirements of the Mental Capacity Act 2005 are met.

Conclusion

So back to our Practice Focus case study, Alan. Should the residential home go down the mental health admission route, or seek to restrict what Alan can do? On the basis of what the legislation says and judicial interpretation of it in the case law above, the best course of action would appear to be as follows:

- Ascertain whether Alan qualifies for detention under the Mental Health Act 1983. Does he have a psychiatric condition which needs to be treated? If so, and he does not agree, does he meet the other statutory criteria in relation to danger to self or others and, for s. 3, is treatment available (ss 2 and 3 Mental Health Act 1983)?
- If the criteria are not met then he could, theoretically, be deprived of his liberty under Schedule A1 Mental Capacity Act 2005.
- If he is to be deprived of his liberty, the first question is whether this would be in his best interests. It goes without saying that all other measures ought to be tried first, the least restrictive option always being preferable.
- If convinced that there is no alternative but to take some kind of drastic action that involves deprivation of liberty, then the home need to ask a BIA to conduct a full assessment as required under the Mental Capacity Act 2005. The next chapter examines exactly what this means.

Further reading

Barber, P, R Brown and D Martin (2012) *Mental Health Law in England and Wales* is a useful overview of mental health legislation. It includes the Mental Health Act 1983 as revised, tribunal requirements and regulations.

Harding, R (2012) 'Legal constructions of dementia: discourses of autonomy at the margins of capacity' 34(4) *Journal of Social Welfare and Family Law* 425–42 is a critical analysis of courts' approach to the Mental Capacity Act 2005 and the right to autonomy for people with dementia. It uses discourse analysis to explore how judges set out making decisions and the implications which, it is argued, constrain autonomy and argues for a more person-centred approach.

Jones, R (2012) *Mental Capacity Act Manual*: comprehensive guidance on the Mental Capacity Act 2005 including Deprivation of Liberty Safeguards of which Jones is highly critical. It is particularly strong on clarifying connections and distinctions between mental health and mental capacity legislation.

Jones, R (2012b) *Mental Health Act Manual*: comprehensive guidance and interpretation of all aspects of mental health legislation. It includes the legislation itself and copious footnotes.

Rapaport, J et al. (2009) 'Mental health and mental capacity law: some mutual concerns for social work' 21(2) *Practice* 91–105 offers an overview of the developments in mental capacity law focusing on distinction between mental capacity and mental health. Specifically, it examines interaction between the Mental Capacity Act 2005 and the Mental Health Act 2007.

5
DEPRIVATION OF LIBERTY

AT A GLANCE THIS CHAPTER COVERS:

- a brief summary of social work law, relating both to children and adults, that includes provision for deprivation of liberty
- an overview of the Mental Capacity Act 2005 Deprivation of Liberty Safeguards
- the distinction between deprivation of liberty and a restriction on liberty
- the Deprivation of Liberty Safeguards and the role of the Best Interests Assessor
- case law relating to the social worker as Best Interests Assessor

This chapter explores an important civil liberties issue, namely in what circumstances someone loses their right to say where they should live or, in relation to children, where their parents provide for them to live. One circumstance obviously relates to arrest, detention and conviction for criminal offences, but here the focus is on deprivation of liberty which has an ultimate purpose or justification as being in someone's best interests.

It is worth reiterating the legal distinction between adults, of 18 years and above, who have absolute rights to liberty unless circumstances apply where the law deems otherwise, and children who have no such rights unless they are accorded such rights by legislation or case law. Chapter 1 summarized how specific case law decisions have extended the rights of young people to make certain kinds of decisions for themselves. In this chapter, there is a summary of ways in which parents lose the rights to decide where their children live, before moving on to consider the range of laws that potentially may apply to vulnerable adults who need to be deprived of their liberty in order to protect them from harm or in some other circumstances where this is deemed to be in their best interests. This consists of two major Acts of Parliament and a residuary role played by the courts exercising their inherent jurisdiction.

Deprivation of liberty: parents and children

Apart from criminal law, which in this context would include Criminal Justice and Immigration Act 2008 provisions for detention and training orders and the Legal Aid Sentencing and Punishment of Offenders Act 2012 remand provisions, the principal legislation concerning parents losing rights over their own children comprises the Children Act 1989 and the Adoption and Children Act 2002. Practitioners in this field will already be familiar with care proceedings but it may be useful to offer a quick résumé of the relevant legislation that diminishes or curtails parental rights:

1 Investigatory processes where there are allegations of children being harmed can include removing children from parental care or preventing parents discharging children from the place where they are being held, for example, from a hospital or foster care home. The key powers here are police powers to make arrangements for accommodation and detain children there to prevent their removal (s. 46 Children Act 1989), and emergency protection orders granted by courts to achieve the same

objective (s. 44). Following on from these emergency orders, courts may grant interim care orders which temporarily transfer parental rights (to say where children should live) to the local authority (s. 38).

2 Where significant harm is proven, courts have the right, in circumstances where they consider it appropriate, to make a care order. The effect of a care order is to grant the local authority a share in parental responsibility for the child (s. 33 Children Act 1989), so, in effect, the local authority decides where the child lives.

3 Other orders made by courts in family proceedings, such as residence orders (s. 8 Children Act 1989), which grant someone the right to say where the child lives to the exclusion of one or both parents, and special guardianship, which permits the **special guardians** to exercise parental responsibility to the exclusion of parents (s. 14C Children Act 1989).

4 Either by agreement, or in the circumstances set out in s. 52 Adoption and Children Act 2002, a child may be adopted and adoption transfers all parental rights to the adopters (s. 46 Adoption and Children Act 2002).

5 For children already accommodated by a local authority there is provision for secure accommodation, where there is a history of absconding alongside the probability of significant harm or injury to themselves or other people (s. 25 Children Act 1989). There are strict time limits, with an absolute maximum of three months (Children (Secure Accommodation) Regulations 1991).

6 The High Court has additional powers to restrict parental decision-making by exercising its inherent jurisdiction or by using its powers of wardship. These derive from common law but are subject to substantial restrictions which do not allow the court, for example, to place a ward of court in the care of a local authority (s. 100 Children Act 1989).

It needs to be said that all of this is subject to compliance with various Articles of the ECHR, most especially Article 8, the right to family life. In care proceedings cases in particular, the extent to which the Article influences the outcome of the case depends on the application of the principle of 'proportionality'. This means that the intended action must be lawful and consistent with its purpose, but not excessive. For example, in *Re T (A Child) (Care Order)* [2009] a child suffered a non-accidental injury and care proceedings were instituted with the local authority eventually recommending care resumed by parents under a supervision order with safeguards. The judge rejected this and made a care order, but the

Appeal Court overturned this decision as not proportionate to the degree of risk, opting instead for the supervision order which was originally recommended.

On-the-spot question	How might this principle of proportionality apply in other kinds of child safeguarding cases?

One example might be where courts are invited to make a placement order with a view of placing the child for adoption (s. 21 Adoption and Children Act 2002). If parents are resistant to this plan courts would obviously have to consider whether divesting the parents of all parental rights would be a proportional response to a finding of significant harm (grounds for a care order which is a prerequisite for the placement order) together with an assessment that said that returning the child to parental care would not be a realistic prospect. How courts would actually assess proportionality was set out in some detail in judgments in *Re B (A Child) (Care Order)* [2013] and *Re B-S (Children) (Adoption: Application of Threshold Criteria)* [2013] which restated that adoption in these circumstances should be a 'last resort' when 'nothing else will do'.

Deprivation of liberty: vulnerable adults

Contrary to popular belief, there is only very limited statutory provision for compelling a vulnerable adult to leave their home or otherwise to deprive them of their liberty in their own interests. What follows therefore is an inclusive list:

1 In emergencies, as well as the best interests provision in the Mental Capacity Act 2005 covered earlier in this book, there is a general police power to enter and search premises for the purpose 'of saving life or limb' (s. 17 (1)(e) Police and Criminal Evidence Act 1984).

2 There is a public health provision in the National Assistance Act 1948 to remove someone from home, by force if necessary, if they are 'suffering from grave chronic disease or, being aged, infirm or physically incapacitated, are living in insanitary conditions' and 'are unable to devote to themselves, and are not receiving from other persons, proper care and attention' (s. 47(1) National Assistance Act 1948). The grounds are that it is in that person's interests or necessary to

prevent injury or nuisance to others. An initial order can be made for up to three months, renewable for further periods of three months at a time (s. 47(3) and (4) National Assistance Act 1948). As mentioned in Chapter 2 this legislation probably breaches human rights law and the Law Commission (2011) has recommended its abolition.

3 As already outlined, the Mental Health Act 1983 sets out statutory criteria for the compulsory admission of people with a mental disorder to hospital. This can only apply where someone has a mental disorder 'of the nature or degree that warrants the detention' and an assessment that the person needs to be detained in the interests of their own health or safety 'or with a view to the protection of other persons' (s. 2 Mental Health Act 1983). This also requires confirmation that this is the least restrictive way of addressing the problems, and for longer-term orders there are additional requirements in relation to treatment availability.

4 Common law provision has included for many years the role of the High Court, using its inherent jurisdiction powers, making orders that protect the most vulnerable. This has traditionally included making financial provision for those who lose capacity to manage financial affairs, making wills in similar circumstances and making medical decisions on behalf of vulnerable adults who do not understand the issues at stake. In some cases the court has authorized use of reasonable force (*Norfolk v Norwich Healthcare (NHS) Trust* [1996]). The *Bournewood* case discussed in Chapter 2 centred on the appropriateness of this common law power, which was considered to fall short of meeting the ECHR requirements in Article 6 (*HL v UK* 2004).

5 Because of the European Court's decision in the *Bournewood* case, the Deprivation of Liberty Safeguards were introduced. These were made a statutory requirement by inserting additions to s. 4 Mental Capacity Act 2005 (s. 50 Mental Health Act 2007). These amendments in turn referred to a new Schedule (A1) Mental Capacity Act 2005 which constitute, in effect, the Deprivation of Liberty Safeguards.

On-the-spot question

Thinking back to Chapter 2, what were the limitations in UK law highlighted by the *Bournewood* case judgment that the Mental Health Act 2007 tried to address by amending the Mental Capacity Act 2005?

The limitations addressed by the Mental Health Act 2007 were outlined in the chart on page 46.

Overview of the Deprivation of Liberty Safeguards

The Deprivation of Liberty Safeguards potentially apply to any adult who falls outside mental health law provisions (for which see Chapter 4) but who has some form of mental disorder connected to their lack of capacity (the meaning of capacity was discussed in the 'Introduction'). The intention of the safeguards is to make a best interests decision on behalf of someone who has lost the ability to make that decision, that decision being specifically in relation to being kept somewhere where the person needs to be cared for or treated. The Deprivation of Liberty Safeguards are formulated on the assumption that the person is already in a care home or hospital and needs to be detained there; they do not apply to people living in their own homes, although the Court of Protection itself does have other powers under s. 16 Mental Capacity Act 2005 that might be appropriate in such cases (see Chapter 6 for further discussion of the role of the Court of Protection). Most of the law relating to this is to be found in the schedules added to the Mental Capacity Act 2005, Schedules A1 and 1A, which in turn relate to s. 4.

Hence the assumption is that the process will be started by the organization that is currently offering care to the patient or resident. In the language of the Deprivation of Liberty Safeguards that is the **Managing Authority**. In the case of patients in hospital the Managing Authority would be the NHS body responsible for running the hospital; in the case of a registered care home the Managing Authority would be whoever runs the home albeit the local authority, voluntary organization or independent body. The procedure is that, when the Managing Authority considers that it might need to deprive someone of their liberty, it applies to a body independent of itself for the authority to do so. Part IV of Schedule A1 Mental Capacity Act 2005 sets out how this should be determined (a brief summary appears in Figure 5.1). It is important to remember that all the principles and provisions already discussed that derive from the Mental Capacity Act 2005 and elsewhere apply, including, critically, the requirement to empower people to make decisions for themselves to the maximum possible extent, and also the requirement that any deprivation of liberty should be proportionate to need.

Hospital or care home requests authorization	• If NHS body is Managing Authority, should apply to the local authority as Supervisory Body • If home in independent sector, should apply to the local authority • If care home run by local authority itself, local authority could apply to an NHS Supervisory Body or to another local authority (Part 4 Schedule A1 Mental Capacity Act 2005)
Supervisory Body asks BIA to assess	• BIA has 21 days counting from day Managing Authority first referrred the case (Mental Capacity (Deprivation of Liberty: Standards Authorisations, Assessments and Ordinary Residents) Regulations 2008) • If in the meantime the Managing Authority needs to deprive someone of their liberty it can issue an urgent authorization itself for a maximum of seven days (Part 5 Schedule A1)
Is it deprivation of liberty?	• Deprivation of liberty as distinct from restriction of liberty • Case law has clarified what this means – see next section of this chapter
Six assessments	• Age = must be 18 years or above • No refusals = deprivation must not conflict with advance decision or wishes expressed on their behalf by an authorized substitute decision-maker • Mental capacity = as defined in ss 1–3 Mental Capacity Act 2005 • Mental health = has mental disorder as defined by s. 1 Mental Health Act 1983 • Eligibility = not potentially subject to compulsory detention under Mental Health Act 1983 • Best interests = necessary to prevent harm to themselves and proportionate
BIA makes recommenda-tions	• Whether deprivation appropriate and proportionate to risk • How long deprivation should be for, up to 12 months • Who should be representative • Whether any conditions should be attached, if so must be related to need for deprivation of liberty
Supervisory Body issues authorization	• Cannot exceed period recommended by BIA • Must appoint representative; if none available consider professional advocate • Must organize reviews either on request or just prior to end of authorization period (Part 8 Schedule A1) • If renewal requested organize another assessment

Figure 5.1: Standard authorization procedure

As soon as the Managing Authority applies, the Supervisory Body appoints a BIA to investigate the case and make recommendations to it as to whether someone should be deprived of their liberty or not. Currently the regulations put in place by s. 129 of Schedule A1 stipulate that a BIA may be a social worker, occupational therapist, nurse or psychologist who has received specific additional training. If the BIA does recommend deprivation of liberty, it is the role of the BIA to recommend the maximum period for which someone should be deprived of their liberty, no more than 12 months, and whether there should be any conditions attached (s. 39 of Schedule A1 Mental Capacity Act 2005). This recommendation has to be on the basis of six assessments, involving at least two assessors, and after full consultation with people involved in the patient's care or treatment. Later this chapter considers what each of these assessments should address. As part of this overall process the BIA needs to recommend a person to be appointed as an advocate or 'representative' for the person who is to be deprived of their liberty. Figure 5.1 may help to elucidate this procedure.

As indicated in Figure 5.1, in an emergency there is a procedure whereby the Managing Authority issues itself with the authority to deprive someone of their liberty, providing that, at the same time, it applies for a standard authorization. For the practitioner this is quite demanding since the assessment process is then constrained to a maximum seven days – although it can be renewed once for a further seven days – beginning on the day on which the Managing Authority initiated the process, which may not, of course, be the day on which the Supervisory Body allocates the task to a BIA.

Before considering how these procedures apply in a particular case, this chapter explores some core principles that underpin the Deprivation of Liberty Safeguards, most especially those that have been clarified and refined in recent case law.

Whilst there are a number of important considerations for the BIA, the crucial first decision concerns whether this really is, in legal terms, a deprivation of liberty and not a permissible restriction of liberty.

What is meant by deprivation of liberty?

There are two key cases here, both of which ended in an appeal to the Supreme Court. The first centred on whether deprivation of liberty within the meaning of Article 5 ECHR occurred in a domestic setting.

> **KEY CASE ANALYSIS** ←

P and Q (MIG and MEG) v Surrey County Council and Others [2014]

Two sisters, P and Q, both have severe learning disabilities. In 2007 care proceedings were instituted when they were 16 and 15. Now they are adults P lives with her former respite carer while Q lives in a residential home.

As neither of them had the capacity to make their own decisions, the Official Solicitor represented them and made an application on their behalf to the court, suggesting that they were being deprived of their liberty because they were unable to decide where they lived, they were not free to leave their placements and they were subject to continuous supervision and control, including restrictions on social contacts (these restrictions originally being authorized by the court under care proceedings).

The Appeal Court agreed that, theoretically, it would be possible for someone to be considered to be deprived of their liberty under Article 5 ECHR even though they were living in a domestic setting. However, the Appeal Court held that it was not deprivation simply on the grounds that the person lacked capacity to decide whether to remain there or not – the consideration had to be wider and look at the whole context. So the Appeal Court concluded that, in these cases, it was not deprivation of liberty given the context (such as the size of the home) and passive consent (they did not object to being where they were). However, the Supreme Court overruled this and declared that it was important not to confuse benevolent justification for the care arrangements with the concept of deprivation of liberty. Human rights are universal and objective; physical liberty is the same for everyone, regardless of their disabilities. What would be a deprivation of liberty for a non-disabled person is also a deprivation for a disabled person (UKSC 19 judgment paras 45–46).

In the next case, the Court of Appeal offered guidance for professionals on distinguishing deprivation of liberty and restriction. There was initially some consternation that the Appeal Court's interpretation meant the end of the Deprivation of Liberty Safeguards but that did not prove to be the case. Furthermore, some of the Appeal Court's views were overruled by the Supreme Court.

> **KEY CASE ANALYSIS**

Cheshire West and Chester Council v P [2014]

This case concerned a man who had Down's syndrome and cerebral palsy. He lived in a four-bed residential unit from which he went out to attend day centres, yet nevertheless he was under close supervision at all times and occasionally had to be restrained to manage his behaviour. The Court of Protection therefore concluded that he was deprived of his liberty since he was 'completely under the control of members of staff'.

The Court of Appeal declared otherwise. That court declared that the restrictions in this case were nothing more than 'the inevitable corollary of his various disabilities' and would be necessary regardless of the environment. The court suggested a 'context and comparator' test whereby the starting point should not be a comparison with an 'ordinary adult going about normal life' but instead, in the case of an adult with disabilities, the comparison should be made with an adult of similar age 'with the same capabilities and affected by the same condition or suffering the same inherent mental and physical disabilities and limitations' (para. 86 of the judgment).

However, the Supreme Court took the view that deprivation of liberty had to be objective and in effect agreed with the Court of Protection.

The Court of Appeal elucidated its reasoning, which was refined and reinterpreted by the Supreme Court, which added its own points of principle.

1 The starting point is what is described as the 'concrete situation'. Deprivation of and restriction of liberty are not two different concepts. The distinction is merely one of degree or intensity, and not one of nature or substance (*Stanev v Bulgaria* [2012] para. 155).
2 Restriction of liberty is not itself a deprivation.
3 Simply not having the capacity to consent to living arrangements is not of itself deprivation of liberty.
4 Someone might be deprived of their liberty without knowing it.
5 Motives are of limited relevance. So it is possible for restriction to become deprivation if there is an improper motive or intention but, likewise 'We should not let the comparative benevolence of the living arrangements with which we are concerned blind us to their essential character if indeed that constitutes a deprivation of liberty.' (*Cheshire West and Chester Council v P* [2014] para. 35)
6 It is always relevant to consider the 'relative normality' of the situation. Relative normality means comparing what is happening to the

'disabled' person compared to other people of a similar age, not people with similar disabilities (para. 47).

7 Ultimately, it is the constraints that matter. Even though the best possible arrangements have clearly been made, they still need to be legally justified.

Having outlined these two key cases, it should now be possible to see whether this elucidation of what constitutes deprivation of liberty helps to make appropriate distinctions in the kinds of cases which are likely to come to the attention of a social worker.

PRACTICE FOCUS

In each of these scenarios consider whether this represents a deprivation of liberty or a restriction.

1 AB, aged 92, lives in a residential home where a number of residents have severe dementia. The front door is locked both day and night. If the resident wants to go out during the day, then this can be arranged if there is a member of staff available. However, if a resident asks to go out at night, they are refused on the grounds that this is unsafe and that staff are not allowed to go out at night with residents.

2 DE, aged 76, had lost his sight and had significant memory impairments as a result of a stroke. His wife became so desperate caring for him at home that she placed him outside on the pavement in order to compel the local authority to organize care for him. Subsequently, DE declared that he wished to return home to his wife but the local authority refused to consider this and, when his wife tried to remove him from the home, the local authority threatened to call the police. At that point she complained of a deprivation of liberty.

3 MN was aged 12 when he was admitted, at the request of his mother, to a psychiatric ward at the hospital. He stayed there for five months and on discharge complained of deprivation of liberty. The door of the ward was locked yet, whilst in hospital, he was free to leave with permission and go out if accompanied by a member of staff.

4 HM, aged 84, was placed in a nursing home following the breakdown of community care arrangements. She and her relatives had not cooperated with care agencies when at home and so she was moved to a nursing home on medical grounds. She was free to move around the home and to maintain social contacts, but nevertheless complained of deprivation of liberty.

In the first case, which is fictitious but reflects standard practice in many care homes, there is indubitably a restriction of liberty, but is it deprivation? The question one might ask is: in what ways is this arrangement different from what most people expect in their own homes? In every respect, the care home arrangements appear reasonable and certainly consistent with the expectations of the kind of response one would make to people with dementia. Comparing the arrangements for AB with anyone else with a similar degree of dementia, one would be bound to conclude that the restriction is reasonable, but the crucial question is, following the Supreme Court's interpretations in *Cheshire West and Chester* (above), whether objectively it is intensive enough to amount to a deprivation of liberty. Ultimately, how does it stand in relation to the reference in the European Court judgment in *HL v UK* [2004] to the 'key factor' being that professionals 'exercised complete and effective control' over HL's care and movements?

The case of DE is a real case (*JE v DE and Surrey County Council* (2006)) in which much hinged on the local authority's refusal to allow DE to return home. The court considered this tantamount to a deprivation of liberty. DE was not free to leave and was totally subject to the control of the local authority which decided where he should live and whether he could be with his wife. The case amply fulfilled the 'complete and effective control' criterion expounded in *HL v UK*. The degree of restriction was certainly sufficient to say that it constituted a deprivation of liberty.

MN is also real, a Danish case considered by the European Court (*Nielsen v Denmark* [1988]) in which it concluded that the arrangements on the psychiatric ward were not much different from the arrangements of any ward in any ordinary hospital. Indeed, they were not far different from the normal arrangements applicable to any 12-year-old, so were not considered a deprivation of liberty. This case has influenced a number of other decisions in similar cases, including *Cheshire West and Chester*, but has been severely criticized in a number of quarters.

HM is also a European Court case, this time from Switzerland (*HM v Switzerland* 2002) in which the court decided that the actions by the Swiss authorities were appropriate and necessary to provide medical care and satisfactory standards of hygiene. The actions were responsible and in HM's best interests. Given that she had considerable freedom within the home and was able to maintain all her social contacts, this was not deprivation of liberty. The determining issue in this case appears to be that there was consent to the original admission, which some might consider dubious.

The critical distinction here is between deprivation and restriction of liberty. Building on the outcomes of some of the decisions made by the European Court of Human Rights, particularly *HL v UK*, the Mental Capacity Act 2005 incorporates provisions that lay down principles and requirements related to both restriction and deprivation of liberty. A restriction of liberty must comply with the general provisions of the Mental Capacity Act 2005 but a deprivation now requires explicit authorization that follows the procedure set out in Figure 5.1 and accords with the revised s. 4 and the additional Schedule A1.

As might be surmised from the two cases highlighted above, there is now a small body of case law related to this issue. Some of this does not just relate to vulnerable adults but also includes children.

For example, in *A Local Authority v A and B* [2010], the court had to consider whether a child and an adult were deprived of their liberty to the extent that this breached Article 5 ECHR. The case had been brought to the court's attention by a local authority concerned that it might be implicated in a deprivation of liberty, and had therefore asked the court to adjudicate on this matter and also to advise about the extent to which the local authority had a responsibility in similar cases. At the time of the court case, the child was aged eight and the adult 22; the fact that the court considered both cases together is remarkable and has drawn some comment (Herring and Dunn, 2011). There was no family connection, but what they had in common was their medical condition known as Smith Magenis syndrome. What they also had in common is that they benefited from devoted and what the court described as 'exemplary' care from their respective parents, such that no one could ever suggest that there should be any criticism of it, and certainly there was no need for any court action regarding this. The only issue for the court to decide was whether the steps the families had taken to provide that exemplary care involved a degree of control that was tantamount to deprivation of liberty. In both cases this involved locking bedroom doors at night so that the person could not endanger themselves. In the case of the child, A, she had a history of turning on the taps in the bathroom, eating soap, turning on the electric oven, eating frozen food, and trying to get out of the house through the garage door. She has no insight into the dangerousness of her behaviour and would persevere with this unless forcibly stopped.

The court concluded that, despite what appear to be apparently extreme measures to control behaviour by confining someone to their bedroom, this did not come anywhere near constituting deprivation of liberty as implied in Article 5 ECHR. The principal reason for this decision is that these steps to control behaviour are a necessary and inevitable consequence of the medical condition. That medical condition involved a combination of learning disabilities, severe sleep disruption and unpredictable behaviour and, given the context of care being beyond reproach, it is difficult to see what other action could be taken. In that sense the action is a necessary restriction of liberty, not a deprivation.

As regards the local authority's concern that it was somehow responsible for oversight of cases where there may possibly be a deprivation of liberty, the judge held that that the local authority in this case was acting as a provider of services. It was there to support the families and it was therefore not responsible for oversight of the case, and specifically was not vulnerable to being sued if there had been an allegation of unlawful deprivation. This last point relates to cases in which local authorities provide services following assessment under the National Health Service and Community Care Act 1990 but would also cover provision of services under Part III Children Act 1989.

It may also be worth noting that a case law decision has made it clear that the court should not consider the right to liberty in Article 5 ECHR as a separate or threshold consideration before considering how the Mental Capacity Act 2005 applies. If practitioners comply with the 2005 Act this effectively takes care of the need to comply with the ECHR for, as a summary of the relevant judgment says:

> The Mental Capacity Act 2005 plainly embraced the principles set out in Article 5, and the Article 5 safeguards were reflected in the 2005 Act regime. (*G v E* [2010])

One case with significant similarities to the *A and C* case, is *R (on the Application of C) v A Local Authority* [2011] (the 'blue room' case). An 18-year-old man, with severe autism and anxiety, learning difficulties and sensory impairment, exhibited challenging behaviour that included aggressive and self-destructive features with a danger of self-harm and harm to carers. As a result the specialist school where he lived had made use of a specially constructed padded 'blue' room with a secure door and window, although the door itself could not be locked. In one month it was used on 192 occasions. On behalf of C it was argued that frequent confinements in this room constituted a deprivation of liberty that breached Article 5 ECHR. In its judgment, the court declared that in deciding whether there was deprivation of liberty under the ECHR three conditions had to be satisfied:

1 There had to be an objective element that someone was confined in a particular restricted place.
2 There had to be a subjective element, meaning that the person had not given a valid consent to the confinement.
3 The deprivation of liberty had to be one for which the state was responsible.

The judgment also referred to the principles that apply to seclusion, drawing on the guidance that is to be found in the *Mental Health Act Code of Practice* (Department of Health, 2008: para. 15.45) which advises that:

1 seclusion should only be used as a last resort and for the shortest possible time;
2 seclusion should not be used as a punishment or a threat, or because of a shortage of staff;
3 it should not form part of a treatment programme; and
4 seclusion should never be used solely as a means of managing self-harming behaviour.

In this particular case, the court concluded that there had been a deprivation of liberty and that there ought to have been some application for its authorization once C attained his 16th birthday – before this birthday it could be considered that child care law applies and therefore parental authority would have been sufficient. The obvious recourse in this case would have been to the Court of Protection which could have authorized the deprivation, but would also have insisted that the use of the blue room be restricted.

This case also serves to highlight the distinctive role of the Court of Protection in that that court can make orders that relate to deprivation of liberty in any setting, whereas the Deprivation of Liberty Safeguards, which involve social workers as BIAs, only apply to residential care homes and hospital or nursing home facilities.

Building on the outcomes of these case decisions, particularly the *Cheshire West and Chester* case, it is possible to clarify the kinds of cases or situations where deprivation of liberty is likely to be considered a real issue.

The precise delineations between what is a restriction in one case and deprivation in another suggest that each case needs to be determined on its merits. There is no 'class' of case where deprivation of liberty matters should be routinely considered. It may also be the case that, whilst rules in a particular home applied to one resident are merely experienced by that particular individual as a restriction, for another they may become a deprivation. In the fictitious example AB above, it is conceivable that if AB were frequently demanding to leave the home at different times of day and night and was consistently refused, this would then be tantamount to complete control of her movements and therefore might be considered a deprivation. In all cases, the overriding question is, following the *P and Q* Supreme Court decision (see above), whether objectively they are deprived of their liberty. If, in this particular case, additional restrictions were to be imposed on this individual to the extent that they lose effective control over their lives, then this may amount to deprivation.

Above all, it is important not to lose sight of the general principles contained in the Mental Capacity Act 2005, and in this regard it is especially important to see whether steps can be taken to convert a deprivation of liberty to a restriction. Both mental health and mental capacity legislation contain clear expectations that the least restrictive options are to be considered and are to be preferred. How this applies in practice is considered in the case study on page 114, which is the sequel to the case study of Alan from Chapter 4. This will serve as an example of how the BIA role plays out in practice.

The Deprivation of Liberty Safeguards and the role of the BIA

The BIA's principal function is to determine whether there is a deprivation and, if so, whether to recommend that this be authorized. In determining this, the BIA is obliged to submit a recommendation based on six assessments. Whilst overseeing the assessment process, the BIA will need to consult with a variety of people, most especially relatives, and in consultation with them should also determine who would be the best person to act as the representative (official advocate) for the 'relevant person' (the person who is potentially being deprived of their liberty).

In the case (outlined on page 114), if Alan is never allowed out of the home in case he goes drinking, this would clearly be complete control over his movements, to quote the phraseology used in a number of cases cited. What happens if he goes out with a relative? Can he go out with a member of staff accompanying him? What exactly is the risk if he does go out? Bear in mind too that any action must be proportionate to the risks identified (proportionate being the key criterion used in the European Convention). Does the problem arise simply because he has one drink, or

> ### PRACTICE FOCUS
>
> Alan, aged 60, featured earlier in this chapter. He has a psychotic illness, history of excessive drinking and memory problems. Now in a care home, he seems oblivious to health and safety issues, is frequently intoxicated and threatening. The initial debate centred on whether to use mental capacity or mental health legislation to control his behaviour.
>
> Initial consultations with the local psychiatric team suggest that readmission to a psychiatric hospital would not be appropriate. Whilst it would for a short time prevent him from drinking, it would not be possible to treat the underlying problems in this way and so it is unlikely that readmission would serve any useful purpose. In addition it is not absolutely clear how he might fulfil the criteria for compulsory detention under the Mental Health Act 1983.
>
> The management of the home therefore decides it will not allow Alan to leave the home to go to the pub, and so as Managing Authority, requests a standard authorization for deprivation of liberty from the Supervisory Body. In accordance with the Mental Capacity Act 2005, the Supervisory Body asks a BIA to investigate and make recommendations.

does it arise because he has several drinks and does not know when to stop? If it is the latter, is it possible to institute other measures to control how much he drinks – for example, by seeking the cooperation of people who are serving him alcohol, or by having staff accompanying him on his visits to the pub? Those are all relevant questions. Some courses of action would not be acceptable, however; for example, not allowing him access to his own money, especially if he had capacity to manage his money. It may well be that the lack of capacity relates only to understanding the harmful consequences of excessive drinking, in which case any restriction or deprivation of liberty must be related to that. For a more detailed discussion of this aspect there is a similar case study which has more of a medical focus to be found in the *Deprivation of Liberty Safeguards Code of Practice* (Ministry of Justice, 2008:54–56).

Having decided that on the surface it would appear that Alan is to some extent currently being deprived of his liberty, the BIA needs to plan the six assessments. Note that the BIA is not able to carry out all these assessments themselves; there must be at least two assessors involved in the whole process. The chart on the next page sets out what is involved in each assessment and who can carry that assessment out.

Assessment	What is being assessed?	Who can assess?	Knowledge required
Age	Ascertain whether 'relevant person' is 18 or over since this is age stipulated by Deprivation of Liberty Safeguards	Anybody whom the Supervisory Body is satisfied is eligible to be a BIA	How to assess age
No refusals	Whether there is already a valid authority that limits or prohibits a deprivation of liberty	Anybody who the Supervisory Body is satisfied is eligible to be a BIA	Mental Capacity Act 2005 especially advance decisions, Lasting Power of Attorney, role of Court of Protection
Mental capacity	Whether someone has capacity to make their own decisions in relation to this particular area of decision-making (see 'Introduction' and ss 1–3 Mental Capacity Act 2005)	Anyone who is eligible to act as a mental health assessor (see box below) or BIA	Familiarity with Mental Capacity Act principles, especially ss 1–5
Mental health	Whether someone has a mental disorder as defined in s. 1 Mental Health Act 1983 as this is a prerequisite for application of Deprivation of Liberty Safeguards	Doctor, either s. 12 Mental Health Act 1983 approved or with three years' post-registration experience in the diagnosis or treatment of mental disorder	Medical qualifications appropriate experience
Eligibility	Whether admission to a psychiatric hospital under an order of the Mental Health Act 1983 would be more appropriate and if the grounds for such detention are met	A mental health assessor who is also a s. 12 doctor, or a BIA who is also an Approved Mental Health Professional	Knowledge of operation and effects of Mental Health Act 1983
Best interests	Whether it is in someone's best interests to be detained, that detention is necessary to prevent harm to themselves and is a proportionate response to the likelihood of suffering harm and its seriousness	Approved Mental Health Professional, social worker, nurse, occupational therapist or chartered psychologist with the skills and experience specified in the regulations and who has attended a course of training as a BIA	How to determine best interests (s. 4 Mental Capacity Act 2005); what the law requires

Table 5.1: The six assessments

Following on from the six assessments, the BIA needs to decide: whether to recommend deprivation of liberty, if so for what period up to a maximum of 12 months; whether to recommend any conditions; and who should represent the interests of the 'relevant person' whilst that deprivation is in force. There are no specific guidelines concerning the length of period to recommend, although the general principle clearly must be for the minimum period necessary. However, the BIA must give reasons for their selection of the time period, and may wish to bear in mind that there is an automatic process for reviewing the deprivation of liberty which means that it will be withdrawn if it is no longer required, but also that if it needs to be renewed there is a procedure for requesting a new authorization (see the *Code of Practice*, Ministry of Justice, 2008: ch. 8). As regards conditions, these must relate to the need for the deprivation of liberty and cannot just simply be aspects of good practice which the BIA would like to see implemented (Ministry of Justice, 2008: paras 4.74 and 4.75). This introduction to the workings of the Deprivation of Liberty Safeguards offers a flavour of what is involved. Further guidance on more specialist literature can be found at the end of this chapter.

To conclude this section, is a summary of the case (see page 117) that highlights areas where social workers acting as BIAs and local authorities may misinterpret their role and act in ways which, in this case, were declared unlawful. This case concerned the alleged misuse of the Deprivation of Liberty Safeguards and underlines the importance of acting lawfully, both with regard to the operation of the Mental Capacity Act 2005 and the Human Rights Act 1998.

On-the-spot question	What would be the implications of this judgment for social work practice?

The court in this case spelt out the implications by declaring some general principles that should apply in cases such as this:

1 Where the local authority and family disagree, the local authority must not use the Deprivation of Liberty Safeguards as a means of getting its own way in determining what should happen and what it considers to be the best interests of the individual concerned.
2 The duty of the local authority is to arrange the provision of support services and if necessary to refer the matter to the Court of Protection where there is a dispute about best interests.

> **KEY CASE ANALYSIS**

Hillingdon v Neary [2011]

This case primarily concerned the actions of the local authority, the London Borough of Hillingdon, and its BIA in the case of Stephen Neary who was aged 21 at the time when, in December 2009, Hillingdon arranged respite care for him. Stephen has autism and severe learning disabilities, requires substantial support and supervision and had been cared for by his father on his own, his mother and father having separated earlier in 2009. The father's illness led to the request for respite care which was initially arranged for two weeks.

After the two-week period was up, the local authority decided not to return Stephen to his father, citing as their reason for doing so Stephen's challenging behaviour. Various incidents occurred that in the local authority's opinion justified this action. Stephen's father tried to insist on Stephen being returned. In April 2010, Hillingdon as the Supervisory Body issued an authorization for deprivation of liberty to itself as the Managing Authority after an incident in which Stephen snatched glasses from a complete stranger. This action was vigorously contested by Mr Neary (Stephen's father); nevertheless it was not until October 2010 that the dispute between Mr Neary and Hillingdon reached the Court of Protection for adjudication.

The issues for the court to consider were:

1 During the period between January and April 2010 before the authorization for deprivation of liberty was issued, was Stephen being unlawfully deprived of his liberty?
2 Were the actions of the local authority compliant with Article 8 ECHR (respect for family life)?

The court concluded that a deprivation liberty had taken place since both Stephen and his father objected to it, and the environment in which Stephen was being kept involved 'total and effective control of Stephen's every waking moment' in somewhere which was not his home. From January to April there had been no authority for doing this, which breached Article 5 ECHR (right to liberty). Even when belatedly there was this authority, there were some breaches of proper procedures in relation to ensuring that the BIA was independent. Furthermore, disregarding the father's views without any lawful authority was a clear violation of Article 8.

3 In all cases the BIA should be independent of the care planning team. It is certainly not acceptable for a BIA to be applying to their own local authority for deprivation of liberty of someone whose care is managed directly by that authority.

4 As the Supervisory Body, the local authority has a duty to scrutinize assessments independently and not just accept them at face value. It cannot just rubber-stamp the BIA recommendation.

5 For the purpose of considering whether someone should be deprived of their liberty, this issue should not be merged or conflated with the issue of where someone should live. They are separate issues.

6 If there is insufficient independence, no advocate appointed along the lines law requires, no effective review, and delay in referring the matter to the Court of Protection, there will also be a clear breach of Article 5 ECHR.

Conclusion

This chapter explored one of the most important civil liberties issues – personal liberty. The law relating to children and vulnerable adults permits the possibility of them being deprived of their liberty on the grounds that it is there in their own interests. It cannot be over-emphasized that such decisions are weighty, given the need both to empower people by protecting them from harm yet also to respect the fundamentally necessary restrictions on state control over people's lives. Social workers cannot escape the fact that, in this context, they represent the state for they make recommendations to family courts concerning care orders, or to Supervisory Bodies for deprivation of liberty under the Mental Capacity Act 2005. In both cases the loss of liberty could be for a significant period so great care must be taken with assessments and recommendations.

As part of the assessment process, social workers acting as BIAs are required to consult with various people but also, critically, to determine whether someone is actually being deprived of their liberty. A number of important judgments shed light on how deprivation of liberty is defined. Other judgments have also clarified what exactly is the role of the social worker acting as a BIA, and here the case of *Hillingdon v Neary* [2011], cited towards the end of the chapter, is instructive. For there is no doubt that the local authority, with honourable intentions, misused its legal authority and perhaps unwittingly the BIA was complicit in this. What this last case underscores is the importance of advocacy as a means of safeguarding service users' interests and this is the starting point for the next chapter, which focuses on legal mechanisms for appointing decision-makers and representatives who play an important role in empowering and safeguarding the rights of vulnerable adults.

Further reading

Brown, R et al. (2009) *The Mental Capacity Act 2005: A Guide for Practice.* An overall guide to the practice aspects of the Mental Capacity Act 2005, especially in relation to Deprivation of Liberty Safeguards (ch. 16).

Care Quality Commission (CQC) (2013) *Monitoring the Use of the Deprivation of Liberty Safeguards in England*: an overview of the operation of Deprivation of Liberty Safeguards in care homes and hospitals. Includes reference to use of Deprivation of Liberty Safeguards in a safeguarding context. Published annually.

Herring, J and M Dunn (2011) 'Safeguarding children and adults: much of a muchness?' 23(4) *Child and Family Law Quarterly* 528–38. Critical commentary on the case *A Local Authority v A and B* [2010] referred to in this chapter.

Hewitt, D (2012) 'Objection, purpose and normality: three ways in which the courts have inhibited safeguarding' 14(6) *Journal of Adult Protection* 280–86. A trenchant critique of some of the judgments in Deprivation of Liberty Safeguards cases, particularly in relation to the notion of the individual's awareness of deprivation, the deprivation's 'benevolent' purpose, and intention of those who deprive someone of their liberty. Includes references to relevant European court cases.

Ministry of Justice (2008) *Deprivation of Liberty Safeguards Code of Practice.* An overview of the requirements of legislation that incorporates clear guidance on practice, with some very useful case examples. This Code of Practice supplements what it describes as the principal Code, the *Mental Capacity Act 2005 Code of Practice* (Department for Constitutional Affairs, 2007).

Williams, V et al. (2012) *Making Best Interest Decisions: People and Processes.* Findings from a comprehensive research project carried out in 2010–2011 focusing on professional practice in relation to best interests decision-making under the Mental Capacity Act 2005 Deprivation of Liberty Safeguards.

6

ADVOCACY AND SAFEGUARDING PEOPLE'S INTERESTS

AT A GLANCE THIS CHAPTER COVERS:

- advocacy for children
- appointing proxy decision-makers for adults including power of attorney
- role of Independent Mental Capacity Advocates and other kinds of advocates and representatives
- the role of the Court of Protection
- resolving disputes in mental capacity cases
- intersection of mental capacity law, common law and safeguarding

What happens when people cannot look after their own interests? This is an important issue for children involved in care proceedings or legal disputes about their care, and for adults who lose the full ability to make decisions for themselves. What happens when vulnerable adults appear to be in need of protection from exploitation or are vulnerable to some kind of financial abuse? What happens when they know they cannot manage their own affairs or want to nominate someone to look after their affairs for them when they are no longer able to do so? Who has the responsibility for representing the interests of vulnerable adults when there are controls placed on their freedom, or when they are confronted with major changes in living arrangements? What happens when there is a dispute between relatives, local authorities and others concerning what may be in someone's best interests? What role do the courts play in all of this?

These are all issues addressed in this chapter. All these questions concern advocacy and safeguarding in the general sense of protecting people's interests. This chapter is not specifically focused on safeguarding from abuse as such, since this is covered elsewhere in this Focus on Social Work Law series and a major issue which a number of texts have addressed (for which see further reading list at the end of the chapter). In this chapter the concern is to focus on the safeguarding of people's interests, more specifically ensuring that their rights to autonomy are respected even though they may have lost the ability to articulate or even to understand their own needs and rights.

Advocacy for children

Whilst the law generally assumes that any property that children own is managed for them by parents, substitute parents, or in exceptional cases a legal trust, there are clearly going to be some occasions where parents' interests are not necessarily the same as the child's.

In social work the children's Guardian plays an important role in family proceedings. Guardians are employed by CAFCASS which was created by ss 11–17 Criminal Justice and Court Services Act 2000. The functions of CAFCASS are to safeguard and promote the welfare of children, give advice to courts in family proceedings, arrange for children to be represented by lawyers and generally provide advice and support for children and families (s. 12 Criminal Justice and Court Services Act 2000). Hence Guardians can be asked to advise and provide reports in applications for residence, contact, specific issue and prohibited steps orders under s. 8 Children Act 1989. They also have a specific role in relation to adoption applications, particularly concerning parental consent. As regards care proceedings, which are the proceedings most likely to involve social workers, Guardians must be appointed when:

- courts are considering making a care or supervision order (ss 33, 35 Children Act 1989);
- courts direct local authorities to assess harm following private law cases (s. 37 Children Act 1989);
- there is an application to discharge or vary a care or supervision order (s. 39 Children Act 1989);
- there is an application for a contact order for a child already subject to a care order (s. 34 Children Act 1989);
- certain other proceedings, such as appeals (s. 41 Children Act 1989).

The Guardian has an important role to play in assessing the case and in arranging the representation of the child or young person in court through a solicitor. They have rights to examine and copy information held by local authorities 'compiled in connection with the making, or proposed making, by any person of any application under this Act with respect to the child' and 'records of, or held by, a local authority which were compiled in connection with any functions which are social services functions ... so far as those records relate to that child' (s. 42 Children Act 1989). The legislation is consistently clear that records that Guardians can copy are only those that relate to the particular child subject to legal proceedings, and outside of those proceedings Guardians have no rights or duties with regard to the child.

The Guardian's role is confined to specified legal proceedings and they do not have a general remit to take cases forward on behalf of children, for example, in cases where children or young people wish to take legal action against local authorities for alleged breach of duty. It may in some cases be appropriate for parents to take action on behalf of their children, for example, in claims for compensation for injuries suffered in an accident. Where this is not appropriate, and the young person is not able to instruct a solicitor themselves, it may be appropriate to refer the matter to the Official Solicitor (appointed under s. 90 Senior Courts Act 1981). The duty of the Official Solicitor is to act as last resort litigation friend or legal representative in court proceedings where children or adults lack decision-making capacity in relation to the proceedings.

It may also be worth noting that the Mental Capacity Act 2005 can apply to financial, property and allied matters for children where there is evidence of incapacity that is expected to last into adulthood (remember this is the one exception to the principle that the minimum age for the Mental Capacity Act 2005 to apply is 16). This would potentially provide some continuity between childhood and adulthood; it could also offer the supervision of the Court of Protection over any Deputies appointed.

Outside of legal proceedings, there are other children's advocates who have a duty to safeguard their interests. For example, Independent Reporting Officers chair the reviews of children looked after by local authorities, monitor their progress and ensure that their wishes and feelings are given due consideration (s. 25B Children Act 1989). If looked after children wish to make a complaint about their care, they have rights to request the support of an advocate (s. 26A Children Act 1989). The IMCA service (see below) may also be available to them.

Appointing proxy decision-makers for adults

> **PRACTICE FOCUS**
>
> Felix's son and daughter-in-law are beside themselves with worry about him living on his own, now that his partner has died. He appears to be very confused about what day of the week it is and seems to be very disorganized and unable to care for himself, despite being a comparatively young older person at the age of 72. He also seems to have completely lost the ability to look after his own financial affairs.
>
> 1 Can his son and daughter-in-law ask someone to look after Felix's financial affairs for him?
> 2 Can they themselves take over managing his affairs?
> 3 Is this a job for a social worker?
> 4 What if Felix won't agree?
> 5 What if he cannot agree, meaning that he has lost the 'capacity' to do so?

The first issue to be addressed is whether, despite his apparent disorganization and confusion, Felix still understands enough to know that he needs help. If this is the case, would he be prepared to agree to someone looking after his financial affairs for him, and if so, which person would he like to nominate?

Nominating someone to look after one's own affairs is comparatively straightforward in the sense that everyone has the right to nominate someone else to do something for them as an agent. Everyday business affairs are conducted in this way. If someone wants to buy car insurance, they may decide to use the services of a broker who can get the best deal, in which case the insurance broker is an agent. Likewise they may choose to arrange a holiday through a travel agent, or buy a house through estate agents who negotiate with the vendor and negotiate part of the transaction for them. In all these cases the agents have a very specific role and legally must not go outside the exact remit, the precise sphere of business transactions delegated to them. What if someone needs somebody to do more than this? What if they need someone to look after their affairs generally, for example, if they decide to work abroad for a short time?

Essentially the same rights apply in that an individual (adult) has the absolute right to delegate looking after business and personal affairs to someone else, in this case such a person will be known as a **donee**, being the person who has been given the authority and power to act, and such an arrangement will be known as a power of attorney. In what follows, this is referred to as an ordinary power of attorney.

The legal principles underpinning power of attorney are quite strict in the sense that it always ought to be possible to check with the donor, the person who gives away or delegates their power, that:

- they have indeed done this;
- that they have a full understanding of what they want the donee to do; and, crucially,
- that they currently have the legal capacity to delegate this power.

As soon as someone loses capacity in relation to the decision to delegate powers, then an ordinary power of attorney simply comes to an end as it cannot continue without this evidence that the donor has capacity.

This is therefore of limited value when it is likely that someone will lose capacity. To overcome this obstacle, the law allows someone to establish a power of attorney on a long-term basis that will persist even though the donor might at some future date lose capacity to delegate the powers. Such an arrangement is known as a Lasting Power of Attorney (ss 9–14 Mental Capacity Act 2005).

So, in this case, if Felix still has some vestige of understanding that he needs to appoint someone to look after his financial affairs then he can do so by completing an application for a Lasting Power of Attorney obtainable from the Office of the Public Guardian. If the son and daughter-in-law want to do it for him, then they must do this with his full agreement and obviously he must have the capacity to delegate at the time when the Lasting Power of Attorney is set up. Naturally, he is under no obligation to nominate them as the donees and, indeed, there are no restrictions on who can be nominated, although for practical reasons the donee would clearly have to agree and be in a feasible position to manage the donor's affairs. Once Felix gets to the stage where he can no longer manage his own affairs and has lost capacity in relation to, for example, financial decision-making, then the arrangement becomes registered and subject to the oversight of the Office of the Public Guardian.

There are in fact two kinds of Lasting Powers of Attorney: personal welfare and property. They are regarded as separate in that it is possible to appoint different donees for the two distinct kinds of Lasting Powers of Attorney, and it is also advisable to appoint more than one for each, to cover circumstances such as an attorney becoming temporarily or permanently unable to carry out the duties. The difference between the two kinds is fairly self-explanatory, but it needs to be clear that in both cases the donee only takes over those aspects of decision-making which are no longer within the capacity of the donor. In addition, the donor can stipulate certain kinds of decisions that the donee may or may not make in the future, and this is particularly important in relation to any advance decisions to refuse treatment which the donor would want to see implemented (advance decisions were discussed in Chapter 3). The principle is that the donee can make decisions regarding treatment and care under the personal welfare Lasting Power of Attorney, but can only make decisions that are not in conflict with an advance decision to refuse treatment. Naturally, the donee should always act in the donor's best interests.

| *On-the-spot question* | What role is there for a social worker in cases where the donee of a Lasting Power of Attorney does not appear to be acting in the donor's interests? |

It is clear that in some cases the donee of a Lasting Power of Attorney will be extensively involved in managing someone's affairs and making decisions on their behalf and for this reason it is not generally a role that is taken on by social workers themselves. There is also the possibility that there may be disagreements about what should happen to someone who is in receipt of services arranged by a local authority, in which case it would clearly be a violation of the principle of independence if it transpired that the social worker acting as donee was also employed by that local authority. If it appeared that the donee of a Lasting Power of Attorney was not always acting in the donor's interests, the social worker would surely have to institute the local authority's safeguarding procedures, which may ultimately involve referral to the Court of Protection.

Questions 4 and 5 in this Practice Focus raise the issue of what to do if Felix does not agree or has lost the capacity to agree to a Lasting Power of Attorney. If this is the case then, whichever it is, the Lasting Power of Attorney route ceases to be viable and recourse must be made to the Court of Protection which has the power to appoint Deputies who can manage people's affairs for them, subject to the oversight of the Public Guardian (ss 16 and 58 Mental Capacity Act 2005). Fees will be payable for these services, so some consideration needs to be made as to whether the assets are substantial enough to justify this.

Role of IMHAs, IMCAs and other kinds of advocates or representatives for adults

In addition to donees of Lasting Power of Attorney and Deputies appointed by the Court of Protection, a number of other sources of advocacy exist in particular circumstances. Chief amongst these is the independent advocacy role which consists of two specialisms: **Independent Mental Health Advocates** (IMHAs) and IMCAs.

IMHAs play a specific role in relation to the operation of the Mental Health Act 1983. They have to be available to certain categories of 'qualifying' patients, primarily those subject to detention. Specifically, s. 30 Mental Health Act 2007 says that such patients are:

- someone detained for longer than 72 hours under a provision of the Mental Health Act 1983, even if on leave of absence;
- someone who is subject to guardianship (s. 7 Mental Health Act 1983);

- someone who is subject to supervised community treatment (s. 17A Mental Health Act 1983);
- an informal patient where certain kinds of treatment are proposed.

IMCAs have a different and slightly wider remit. The role was introduced by the Mental Capacity Act 2005 (ss 35–41). The purpose of the role is to ensure that there is someone who speaks for an adult who is not able to speak for themselves, most especially with regards to important decisions made in their lives. Hence they should always be appointed where someone does not have family or friends who can represent their interests, and in some circumstances will be available for consultation by friends and family. There are certain circumstances in which an IMCA must be appointed for people who may not have capacity and who have no one else to represent them:

- where an NHS body is proposing to provide serious medical treatment for someone and that person lacks capacity to consent to treatment (s. 37 Mental Capacity Act 2005). This obviously excludes cases more appropriate for IMHAs but does include a very wide range of treatments (examples will be found in the *Mental Capacity Act 2005 Code of Practice*, Department for Constitutional Affairs, 2007: para. 10.45). Serious treatment includes 'providing, withdrawing or withholding treatment' in circumstances where there is a fine balance between benefits and risks, a fine balance about choice, or when that treatment may involve serious consequences (s. 4(2) Mental Capacity Act 2005 (Independent Mental Capacity Advocates) (General) Regulations 2006);
- where an NHS body proposes to provide accommodation in hospital or a care home, or change that accommodation (s. 38 Mental Capacity Act 2005);
- where a local authority proposes to provide residential accommodation or change that person's residential accommodation (s. 39 Mental Capacity Act 2005);
- where an NHS body or a local authority is planning measures to protect a vulnerable adult (this is a permissive power under the Mental Capacity Act 2005 (Independent Mental Capacity Advocates) (Expansion of Role) Regulations 2006);
- where there is an application for authorization for deprivation of liberty (see Chapter 5) (s. 39A Mental Capacity Act 2005).

Note that in all the cases above the IMCA will only generally be appointed where there is no one else to safeguard the interests of the person concerned. However, there is one important exception to this principle: an IMCA may be appointed where there is a safeguarding investigation (s. 4 Mental Capacity Act 2005 (Independent Mental Capacity Advocates) (Expansion of Role) Regulations 2006). This can apply even if there are friends and family in circumstances where it would be beneficial to the person concerned.

In relation to authorizations for deprivation of liberty that are implemented, the Supervisory Body must appoint a representative to advocate for the 'relevant person' – that is the person subject to the deprivation – by maintaining contact with them and representing them in reviews, initiating any complaints or in making an application to the Court of Protection (Ministry of Justice, 2008: ch. 7). As explained in Chapter 5, it is the duty of the BIA to ascertain who is the best person to be appointed as representative and to nominate them to the Supervisory Body. Once appointed, both the representative and the person deprived of liberty under a standard authorization have a right of access to an IMCA, and it is the duty of the Supervisory Body to arrange this, if requested. The role of the IMCA in these circumstances is to:

> assist the relevant person and their representative to understand the effect of the authorization, what it means, why it has been given, and why the relevant person meets the criteria for authorization, how long it will last, any conditions to which the authorization is subject and how to trigger a review or challenge in the Court of Protection.
>
> *Ministry of Justice, 2008: para. 7.38*

These arrangements do not apply if the representative is a professional advocate or where there is already a donee or a court-appointed Deputy.

The IMCA has the right to interview the person for whom they are an advocate in private and also has the right to examine and copy health records, local authority records and care home records were these are considered relevant to the advocacy (s. 35 Mental Capacity Act 2005). Further information on how the IMCA should carry out their role is covered in regulations, principally the Mental Capacity Act 2005 (Independent Mental Capacity Advocates) (General) Regulations 2006.

In cases which involve court proceedings, the role of the Official Solicitor is quite important, since the Official Solicitor may be called upon to represent the interests of people who are unable to instruct solicitors themselves. Just as with children, the role is to act as a last resort litigation friend or lawyer, so in a number of mental capacity cases the Official Solicitor has represented the interests of the person concerned. The Official Solicitor can also be asked by the Court of Protection, in last resort cases, to act as a property and affairs Deputy for individuals. Likewise there is another office, the **Public Trustee** (appointed under s. 8 of the Public Trustee Act 1906) who can act as last resort executor or administrator or trustee in property cases.

The role of the Court of Protection

Throughout this book there been numerous references to the Court of Protection and experienced practitioners will already be familiar with its existence. However, it may be worth summarizing its role in relation to the kinds of dilemmas which social workers in adult care sometimes face.

The Court of Protection has existed for many years but was effectively relaunched by the Mental Capacity Act 2005 (ss 15–23) which extended its role. As a consequence, the court is now the final decision-making body on many matters in relation to people who may have lost capacity. It decides ultimately whether someone does have capacity or does not. It adjudicates on disputes about who has responsibility and how this should be exercised. It can make decisions regarding financial or welfare matters, as has been seen in some of the cases summarized in this book.

The court can appoint a Deputy to act for people who have lost capacity to make decisions for themselves and this is important as the Deputy has ongoing responsibility but is always accountable to the court; and Deputies can be removed and replaced if they fail to carry out their duties. A Deputy could be a family member or friend, or could be a professional person, such as a solicitor or accountant. In some cases it could be appropriate for the local authority to be the Deputy but this would to some extent depend on the willingness of the local authority to take on these kinds of responsibilities. As there are costs involved in the appointment of Deputies, it is only really likely to be feasible to appoint them where financial affairs are more complex than usual. Where someone's income is just statutory benefits then appointeeship, where someone simply collects and disburses the money on behalf of the person who lacks capacity, would be more appropriate.

In relation to Lasting Power of Attorney (and its predecessor the Enduring Power of Attorney) the court can decide whether the power is valid and can arbitrate in cases where there are disputes about how it is put into effect. The responsibility for registering Lasting Powers of Attorney lies with the Office of the Public Guardian, which also oversees management of Deputies and the appointment of Court of Protection Visitors. These Visitors, either general or professionally qualified specialists, provide independent advice to the Court of Protection and Public Guardian and might be appointed where there is absolutely no one else to oversee the well-being of particular individuals. Their prime responsibility is to ensure that the needs of a person who is unable to take responsibility for themselves are addressed by care providers and others. They have rights to inspect health and social care records (s. 61 Mental Capacity Act 2005).

As previously noted, the Court of Protection oversees the operation of the Deprivation of Liberty Safeguards and in this sense acts as a kind of Court of Appeal where people, such as Stephen Neary's father (*Hillingdon v Neary* [2011] case summarized at the end of Chapter 5), object to the actions of a Supervisory Body.

Finally, the Court of Protection is specifically charged with making decisions about whether someone does or does not have capacity in relation to particular decisions and whether actions taken on their behalf are lawful (s. 15 Mental Capacity Act 2005). This clearly puts it in the role of arbiter in cases where there are disputes about capacity and autonomy. The court itself can also make decisions about what is in someone's best interests were a person lacks capacity in relation to particular kinds of decisions. This can relate both to financial and personal welfare matters. Furthermore, the court has a particular role in arbitrating in disputes about what is in the vulnerable person's best interests. Some examples of this follow.

Resolving disputes in mental capacity cases

Cases discussed here differ as regards circumstances, but all involve questions about the extent to which someone has the capacity to make decisions for themselves in the context of some kind of dispute with the local authority.

→ **KEY CASE ANALYSIS** ←

Re F (Vulnerable Adult) (Capacity: Jurisdiction to Make Order on Vulnerable Adult's Behalf) [2009]

There was serious concern about a vulnerable adult's well-being and the Court of Protection acted to decide whether, on these grounds, that person could be deemed to have lost capacity.

F was aged 52 and as a result of significant physical disabilities was effectively bed-bound. Although the local authority provided community care services, it found doing so very difficult because of F's attitude. She was described as antagonistic. Consequently, the local authority reduced care to an absolute minimum, which left some needs unmet. There were also major concerns about F's mental health.

When the case was first heard by the courts, the judge decided that the Mental Capacity Act 2005 started with a presumption of capacity and, in order to take over any decision-taking powers, there had to be evidence of the service user's lack of capacity before considering anything else. The judge concluded that in this case there was no such clear evidence and therefore declined to make an order.

However, the Court of Protection decided that the test the judge applied was not the correct one. The Court of Protection declared that the first consideration ought to be whether there was evidence of real concern that an individual might lack capacity in some respect. Next it had to be considered what would be an appropriate course of action that would be in that person's best interests, which might of course include some safeguarding measures. That course of action then needed to be considered in relation to what someone like F was saying about it. So, in this case, there was a distinct possibility that F lacked capacity in relation to some kinds of decisions concerning her care needs and therefore the court had to make a ruling.

The overall principle was that the individual's right to autonomy of decision-making should be restricted as little as possible, but that this had to be consistent with the person's best interests.

One significant implication of this case decision is that it refutes utterly the idea that the first consideration is whether someone generally has lost capacity, and only after making that decision can one then look at the areas of their lives that cause concern. There are not two categories of people: those who have capacity and those who do not. Instead, practitioners and judicial decision-making bodies must start with the decision itself which someone needs to make and then consider whether someone has the capacity, as defined in the Mental Capacity Act 2005, to make that particular decision in that particular circumstance. Hence, in this case everything hinged on whether F had the capacity to make decisions about her care needs.

Another implication of the case is that it is perfectly appropriate and proper to involve the Court of Protection in deciding a case where there is a dispute between a service user and the local authority, as coordinator of community care services and safeguarding agency, as to what should happen.

In *LBL v RYJ and BJ* [2010] there was dispute about the placement of a young person with significant learning disabilities, but here the capacity issues are somewhat different. The case concerned an 18-year-old who had epilepsy and what were described as significant learning disabilities. Her mother disagreed with the placement arranged by the local authority and objected to the young person spending weekends with an aunt. She also believed that her daughter lacked the capacity to make decisions about placement and contact with family members and asked the Court of Protection to declare that she did not have capacity in relation to those kinds of decisions, presumably with a view to the court agreeing with the mother's views which she would then have the right to impose as being in the daughter's best interests. An independent social worker confirmed that the young woman had mental capacity in relation to those kinds of decisions, but the mother argued that this view was flawed since the daughter could not confirm her views consistently. However, the court held that consistency was not the correct test, since lack of capacity was allegedly demonstrated by continual repetitive questioning failing to elicit exactly the same answer. In this case, it was being assumed that the young person did not have capacity but careful interviewing revealed that she did in relation to certain key decisions. Consistency was not itself grounds for arguing that the young person lacked capacity in relation to decisions about placements and family contacts.

It is clear from this case that the court accepts that, even though someone may have significant learning disabilities, nevertheless they can have capacity in relation to some important areas in their lives. In no way should the severity of disability automatically lead to an assumption that someone is incapable of making any kind of decision.

On the surface, the outcome of this case may appear to be inconsistent with the key case above and other similar cases, but here there was no question of mental health problems or other factors impeding the young person's ability to make decisions. The only real issue was the severity of the learning disability and how to determine whether someone really understands.

Intersection of mental capacity law, common law and safeguarding

It is important to emphasize that mental capacity legislation does not itself address safeguarding in the sense of protecting people from abuse. Adult safeguarding is primarily addressed through policy guidance with no specific legislation, in England and Wales at least, that addresses protection of vulnerable adults from physical and other forms of harm. In England the current guidance is entitled *No Secrets* (Department of Health and the Home Office, 2000). In Wales the guidance is *In Safe Hands* (Welsh Assembly Government, 2000). By complete contrast in Scotland there is specific legislation, the Adult Support and Protection (Scotland) Act 2007 (obviously not included in this book which covers England and Wales only) and there is some suggestion that a similar law might be appropriate in England and Wales (Law Commission, 2011). The more general provisions regarding safeguarding are covered in another book in this series and in the more specialist literature (see further reading at the end of this chapter).

In practice, unsurprisingly, there are occasionally cases where there is concern both about someone's capacity to make decisions for themselves and also about the potential for them being abused by other people. There may also be accusations about relatives not always making decisions in the best interests of the person who has lost capacity, but rather in their own self-interests. In such cases the Court of Protection may play a very useful role.

In safeguarding cases the court may well decide to use its jurisdiction under common law in combination with the Mental Capacity Act 2005 and the ECHR in order to determine what should be done. This may apply where there are safeguarding issues even if the vulnerable adults concerned still have capacity to make their own decisions, as is now clear from the following Court of Protection case.

> **KEY CASE ANALYSIS**

A Local Authority and Others v DL [2012]

In this particular case a son's behaviour towards his parents was tantamount to abuse, yet the parents would not themselves institute any kind of legal proceedings, despite having the capacity to do so. The son lived with his parents and controlled them by physical and verbal threats, deciding when they should go in and out of their house, and restricting visits from health and social care staff. There were also allegations that he was trying to coerce his father into converting the ownership of the house into his name.

An independent social work expert concluded that the son's behaviour compromised the extent to which his parents had capacity to make decisions regarding their living arrangements and personal relationships.

The central issue, according to one judge, was whether the court could put protective measures in place:

> in relation to vulnerable adults who do not fall within the Mental Capacity Act 2005 but who are, or are reasonably believed to be, for some reason deprived of the capacity to make the relevant decision, or disabled from making a free choice, or incapacitated or disabled from giving or expressing a real and genuine consent by reason of such things as constraint, coercion, undue influence or other vitiating factor (*A Local Authority and Others v DL* [2012] [10] citing previous judgment).

It was strongly argued in court that the Court of Protection can only intervene in cases like this where there is evidence that someone lacks mental capacity. Thus in this case the court would have no right to go beyond the Mental Capacity Act 2005.

The court rejected this argument. It decided that there were cases that fell outside the Mental Capacity Act 2005 and there is no legislation that stops the court using its common law powers to intervene in cases where it considered that it ought to protect a vulnerable person (its inherent jurisdiction as it is usually described in legal textbooks). Therefore, in this case, it would have the right to make appropriate orders if needed.

This establishes an important principle: the Court of Protection will get involved in cases where there are serious safeguarding issues even if those who are abused have capacity but will not take action to protect themselves. Such cases will not come under the Mental Capacity Act 2005 but will still fall within the court's jurisdiction using common law powers.

On-the-spot question	In what sorts of scenarios might this also apply?

Intimidation, threats of violence, and threats to withdraw support services for people who are utterly dependant on them might be examples of actions that raise the possibility that someone who apparently has capacity to make decisions is nevertheless impeded from doing so. In extreme cases this will be tantamount to reclassifying someone as not having capacity in relation to specific kinds of decisions.

The final case to be considered in this chapter (see page 136) involves a rather different aspect of common law relating to the extent to which reasonable force can be used to impose care on someone. Practitioners often ask about use of coercion and, whilst it is not such a major issue in social work as it is in healthcare, it is an issue on which the courts have adjudicated. In this case, the court concluded that autonomy did not trump welfare. Yet one might also say nor does welfare trump autonomy. What matters is a balance between the two.

What is interesting about this case is that it sets down threshold criteria that justify use of force but ultimately authorizes 'force or restraint' where the circumstances warrant it. The court specifically referred both to the best interest checklist (for which see chapter 4) and the proportionality principle which derives from the ECHR. This principle of proportionality recurs right through decision-making in relation to both vulnerable adults and children and therefore could legitimately be considered to be the yardstick by which the acceptability of professional practice is governed.

Conclusion

Ultimately, that is the message of this book: autonomy and welfare needs have to be balanced. Autonomy is an important principle that is undergirded by the law, both UK law and the ECHR. In the case of both children and adults, where there are overriding welfare considerations, it

> **KEY CASE ANALYSIS**

Dorset County Council v EH [2009]

This case concerned a woman aged 82 with Alzheimer's who lacked capacity regarding decisions about health, care and risk. Consequently, she had been refusing community care services. The community mental health team concluded that she was not safe in her own home where she lived alone.

The local authority asked the court to confirm that she lacked capacity to make decisions about where she should live and that it was in her best interests to enter secure residential accommodation despite her objections. Further, the local authority asked for confirmation that it was legal to use reasonable force in order to transport EH to the care home and to prevent her from leaving that home if she tried to do so.

On her behalf, the Official Solicitor argued that the risks were insufficient to justify deprivation of liberty, that there was a risk to her autonomy and thereby an infringement of her rights under Article 5 ECHR. The court rejected this argument and decided:

1 EH did lack capacity regarding decisions about her care and well-being.
2 The court did have power to authorize detention in a care home providing this was authorized in advance, that the individual concerned lacked capacity and that the detention was appropriate, there was provision for review, and was supported by medical opinion.
3 The court could authorize force or restraint, which had to be to the minimum degree necessary.
4 Court decisions would always have to comply with the principles of necessity and proportionality. For this purpose the *Mental Capacity Act 2005 Code of Practice* provided a useful checklist (Department for Constitutional Affairs, 2007).
5 The quality of public care had to be at least as good as care currently provided.
6 It was recognized that in this case it would be necessary to order that EH should be in a locked care home and not allowed out without supervision. However, this was proportionate to the likelihood of her suffering harm and although it was a deprivation of liberty it was justified as proportionate.
7 Although it was an important principle, autonomy did not trump welfare.

is possible to contravene this principle providing that clear legal grounds can be substantiated for doing so. In the case of children, the key phrase is 'significant harm', as in s. 31 Children Act 1989. For adults, issues are more complex but principally revolve around the issue of capacity, that is people's ability to make decisions for themselves. Here the Mental Capacity Act 2005 is by far and away the most important aspect of legislation with its systematic definition of capacity, clarification of binding decisions that people can make in advance, and provision for precise processes whereby any breach of autonomy has to be justified as being in someone's best interests. Social workers are daily involved in decisions about what is in people's best interests and are constantly balancing rights to autonomy with welfare needs. This book has attempted to elucidate how social workers are enabled to carry out that balancing act and empower people by respecting rights to autonomy, but also in some cases overriding that autonomy and making a decision that ultimately is for that person's benefit. Autonomy, indeed, does not always trump welfare.

Further reading

Brammer, A (2012) 'Inside the Court of Protection' 14(6) *Journal of Adult Protection* 297–301 offers a succinct overview of the Court of Protection, its development and role. It also highlights some of the issues that are of current concern, for example, privacy and secrecy.

Department for Constitutional Affairs (2007) *Mental Capacity Act 2005 Code of Practice*. There is a useful worked-through case example relevant to Lasting Power of Attorney (74, para 5.17).

Mandelstam, M (2013) *Safeguarding Adults and the Law* is a comprehensive guide to the law specifically in relation to safeguarding, which includes the regulatory framework that governs appointment of staff.

Mantell, A and T Scragg (2011) *Safeguarding Adults in Social Work* is an overview of social work practice issues in relation to safeguarding generally.

Ministry of Justice (2008) *Deprivation of Liberty Safeguards Code of Practice*: ch. 10 has more information on the Court of Protection in relation to Deprivation of Liberty Safeguards.

Redley, M et al. (2011) 'Introducing the Mental Capacity Advocate (IMCA) Service and the reform of adult safeguarding procedures' 41 *British Journal of Social Work* 1058–69: this article offers an overview of the development of adult safeguarding and the role of IMCAs. It presents findings of research into the role of IMCAs in safeguarding and the challenges that result from this.

USEFUL WEBSITES

Department of Health
The Department of Health main website is now at www.gov.uk/government/organisations/department-of-health. However, for access to the Deprivation of Liberty Safeguards Code of Practice, see http://webarchive.national archives.gov.uk/20130107105354/http:/www.dh.gov.uk/en/Publicationsand statistics/Publications/PublicationsPolicyAndGuidance/DH_085476.

Ministry of Justice
For the Mental Capacity Act 2005 generally including the Code of Practice and the role of the court of protection: www.justice.gov.uk/protecting-the-vulnerable/mental-capacity-act.

The Ministry of Justice website also hosts the Office of the Public Guardian's useful website that sets out the procedures for people to follow when they wish to set up a Lasting Power of Attorney, and also acts as a gateway to the Court of Protection: www.justice.gov.uk/about/opg.

Social Care Institute for Excellence
For the SCIE's guide to the role of IMCAs, see: www.scie.org.uk/publications/imca/index.asp. The SCIE also has an excellent section dedicated to safeguarding adults on this link: www.scie.org.uk/adults/safeguarding/index.asp; and an overview of the Mental Capacity Act 2005: www.scie.org.uk/publications/elearning/mentalcapacityact.

GLOSSARY

Active consent
Explicit statement from someone that they agree to a decision or course of action, see exercise in Chapter 3.

Advance decision
Declaration by someone who anticipates that they may lose capacity concerning specific forms of treatment or care which they do not wish to have. It cannot override statute law or authorize action that would directly end someone's life. It can only authorize withdrawal of treatment that might otherwise keep someone alive.

Advocacy
Speaking for people in the sense of articulating exactly what that person says and wants.

Age of criminal responsibility
Age at which children can be held accountable for their actions in law, currently ten in England and Wales.

Approved Mental Health Professionals
Professionals appointed under Mental Health Act 2007 after further training who are empowered to make applications for detention under the Mental Health Act 1983 and are involved in certain other mental health decisions.

Autonomy
Freedom, self-sufficiency and independence.

Best interests
A phrase used in s. 4 Mental Capacity Act 2005 as the criterion for making decisions on behalf of other people. It is explained further in the *Mental Capacity Act 2005 Code of Practice.*

Best Interest Assessor
Role introduced by Deprivation of Liberty Safeguards for person who recommends to Supervisory Body whether someone should be deprived of their liberty.

***Bournewood* gap**
Gap in law identified in this European Court case (*HL v UK* [2004]) in that law failed to provide adequate provision for decisions to be made on behalf of people with learning disabilities and vulnerable adults who had lost the capacity to consent to medical treatment or care, for full explanation see Chapter 2 Table 2.3 and discussion.

CAFCASS
Children and Family Court Advisory and Support Service (created by ss 11–17 Criminal Justice and Court Services Act 2000).

Capacity
People's ability to make decisions for themselves and be accountable for their actions, see the 'Introduction' for fuller explanation.

Care proceedings
Family court proceedings to protect children from 'significant harm' under Part IV Children Act 1989.

Code of Practice
Government official guidance on practice and interpretation of law – for example, *Mental Capacity Act 2005 Code of Practice* (Department for Constitutional Affairs, 2007), *Mental Capacity Act 2005 Deprivation of Liberty Safeguards Code of Practice* (Ministry of Justice, 2008) – not legally binding.

Common law
Law that is not written down but has become accepted law over a lengthy period of time, as agreed by judges in case law interpretations.

Court of Protection
Body established to decide on matters that concern people who have lost capacity, protecting their interests; under the Mental Capacity Act 2005 it has specific responsibilities as explained in Chapter 6.

Deprivation of Liberty Safeguards
Set of rules and regulations introduced by the Mental Health Act 2007 as amendment to the Mental Capacity Act 2005 which set out procedures and

criteria for someone to be compelled to stay in hospital or care home, covered in full in Chapter 5.

Deputy
Someone appointed by the Court of Protection to make decisions on behalf of a person who lacks capacity to make particular decisions.

Derogation
ECHR term that refers to occasions when a legislative body declares that it knows that the Convention may be breached, e.g. in the UK it applies to some aspects of anti-terrorism legislation.

Donee
Someone appointed under Lasting Power of Attorney who can make decisions within the scope of that power on behalf of someone else (the donor).

Empowerment
Action that enhances people's ability and opportunities to speak for themselves and/or to make their own decisions or have decisions taken that are in their best interests.

European Convention on Human Rights
Pan-European rules concerning the relationship between the individual and the state, consists of a number of Articles with adjudication by the European Court of Human Rights in Strasbourg, implemented in the UK principally by the Human Rights Act 1998 which compels public bodies to conform to the Convention.

Fluctuating capacity
Acknowledgment that capacity can vary between days and between different times of day, relevant to s. 3 Mental Capacity Act 2005 concerning decision-making, and referred to in both the Mental Capacity Act 2005 and Deprivation of Liberty Safeguards Codes of Practice (Department for Constitutional Affairs, 2007; Ministry of Justice, 2008).

Guardian
Children's guardian appointed by court in children's cases to assess case, advise them and represent child's interests in court (ss 41, 42 Children Act 1989), usually employed by CAFCASS.

Hybrid organization
Body that exercises both public and private functions, for example, a housing association that has private tenants but also has public law obligations under social housing legislation.

Independent Mental Capacity Advocate
See Chapter 6.

Independent Mental Health Act Advocate
See Chapter 5.

Inherent jurisdiction
Long-standing, historically based power of courts to take action in certain kinds of circumstances, based on common law but can be restricted by statute law.

Lasting Power of Attorney
Arrangement whereby someone can nominate someone else to look after their financial affairs and/or take health or welfare decisions for them after such time as they lose the capacity to decide for themselves (ss 9–14 Mental Capacity Act 2005).

Managing Authority
Person or body responsible for hospital or care home where someone is, or may become, deprived of their liberty (see Chapter 5).

Margin of appreciation
ECHR recognition that each country will have slightly different interpretations of the Convention.

Mental disorder
Term used widely in mental health and mental capacity legislation, definition is to be found in s. 1 Mental Health Act 1983 updated by Mental Health Act 2007, see also Chapter 4.

Nearest relative
Specific role under the Mental Health Act 1983 relating to compulsory admission and detention (ss 26–30 Mental Health Act 1983).

Passive consent
Lack of objection to a decision or course of action, someone does not actually say 'yes' but does not actively resist treatment or being taken somewhere, see Chapter 3 exercise.

Proportionality
Requirement that action to deprive someone of their liberty should directly correlate to the need to deprive and should not be excessive. It is an important consideration in Mental Capacity Act 2005 case law as explained in Chapter 6.

Public Guardian
Organization with administrative responsibilities under Mental Capacity Act 2005, as explained further in Chapter 6.

Public Trustee
Organization with very specific responsibilities in relation to wills and trusts, see Chapter 6.

Reservation
The ECHR allows for reservation of a very specific area where a country acknowledges that its laws do not conform to the Convention.

Residence orders
Orders under s. 8 Children Act 1989 concerning where a child should ordinarily live.

Special guardianship
Authority for someone to look after someone else's child and be granted parental rights over the child, alternative to adoption but without permanency for life (s. 115 Adoption and Children Act 2002 as amended).

Statute law
Law that is written down, e.g. Act of Parliament.

Supervisory Body
Body responsible for considering and authorizing requests from Managing Authorities for deprivation of liberty and for appointing BIAs to advise them (see Chapter 5).

REFERENCES

Adams, R (2008) *Empowerment, Participation and Social Work* 4th edn (Basingstoke: Palgrave Macmillan)

Banks, S (2012) *Ethics and Values in Social Work* 4th edn (Basingstoke: Palgrave Macmillan)

Barber, P, R Brown and D Martin (2012) *Mental Health Law in England and Wales: A Guide for Mental Health Professionals* 2nd edn (London: Sage)

Bartlett, P (2008) *The Mental Capacity Act 2005* 2nd edn (Oxford: Oxford University Press)

British Association of Social Workers (2012) *BASW Code of Ethics* (Birmingham: Venture Press)

Booth, T and W Booth (2004) *Parents with Learning Difficulties, Child Protection and the Courts: A Report to the Nuffield Foundation* (Sheffield: University of Sheffield)

Booth, T, W Booth and D McConnell (2006) 'Temporal discrimination and parents with learning difficulties in the child protection system 36(6) *British Journal of Social Work* 997–1015

Brammer, A (2012) 'Inside the Court of Protection' 14(6) *Journal of Adult Protection* 297–301

Brammer, A (2013) *Social Work Law* 3rd edn with update (London: Pearson)

Brayne, H and H Carr (2013) *Law for Social Workers* 12th edn (Oxford: Oxford University Press)

Brown, R (2013) *The Approved Mental Health Professionals' Guide to Mental Health Law* 3rd edn (London: Sage)

Brown, R, P Barber and D Martin (2009) *The Mental Capacity Act 2005: A Guide for Practice* 2nd edn (London: Sage)

Care Quality Commission (CQC) (2013) *Monitoring the Use of the Deprivation of Liberty Safeguards in England* www.cqc.org.uk/public/publications

Cave, E (2011) 'Maximisation of minors' capacity' 23(4) *Child and Family Law Quarterly* 431–49

Chico, V and L Hagger (2011) 'The Mental Capacity Act 2005 and mature minors, a missed opportunity?' 33(2) *Journal of Social Welfare and Family Law* 157–68

Dalrymple, J and B Burke (2006) *Anti-Oppressive Practice, Social Care and the Law* 2nd edn (Buckingham: Open University Press)

Department for Constitutional Affairs (2007) *Mental Capacity Act 2005 Code of Practice* (Norwich: The Stationery Office)

Department of Health (2008) *The Mental Health Act Code of Practice* (London: Department of Health)

Department of Health and the Home Office (2000) *No Secrets: Guidance on Developing and Implementing Multiagency Policies and Procedures to Protect Vulnerable Adults from Abuse* (London: The Stationery Office)

Director of Public Prosecutions (2010) *Policy for Prosecutors in Cases of Encouraging or Assisting Suicide* (London: Crown Prosecution Service) www.cps.gov.uk

Fovargue, S (2013) 'Doctrinal incoherence or practical problem? Minor parents consenting to their offspring's medical treatment and involvement in research in England and Wales' 25(1) *Child and Family Law Quarterly* 1–18

Freeman, M (2011) *Human Rights* 2nd edn (Cambridge: Polity Press)

Gilmore, S and J Herring (2011) 'No is the hardest word: consent and children's autonomy' 23(1) *Child and Family Law Quarterly* 3–25

Harding, R (2012) 'Legal constructions of dementia: discourses of autonomy at the margins of capacity' 34(4) *Journal of Social Welfare and Family Law* 425–42

Health and Care Professions Council (2012) *Standards of Proficiency for Social Workers in England* (London: HCPC)

Herring, J and M Dunn (2011) 'Safeguarding children and adults: much of a muchness?' 23(4) *Child and Family Law Quarterly* 528–38

Hewitt, D (2012) 'Objection, purpose and normality: three ways in which the courts have inhibited safeguarding' 14(6) *Journal of Adult Protection* 280–86

HM Government (2005) *Mental Capacity Act 2005 Explanatory Notes* (Norwich: The Stationery Office)

Hoffman, D and J Rowe (2003) *Human Rights in the UK* (London: Pearson)

Johns, R (2011) *Using the Law in Social Work* 5th edn (London: Sage)

Jones, R (2012) *Mental Capacity Act Manual* 5th edn (London: Sweet & Maxwell)

Law Commission (1993) *Mentally Incapacitated Adults and Decision-Making: A New Jurisdiction* Consultation Paper 128 (London: HMSO)

Law Commission (2011) *Adult Social Care* http://lawcommission.justice. gov.uk/docs/lc326_adult_social_care.pdf

Lord Chancellor's Department (1997) *Who Decides? Making Decisions on Behalf of Mentally Incapacitated Adults* (London: HMSO)

Lord Chancellor's Department (1999) *Making Decisions* (London: HMSO)

MacIntyre, G and A Stewart (2011) 'For the record: the lived experience of parents with a learning disability – a pilot study examining the Scottish perspective' 40 *British Journal of Learning Disabilities* 5–14

Mandelstam, M (2013) *Safeguarding Adults and the Law* 2nd edn (London: Jessica Kingsley)

Mantell, A and T Scragg (2011) *Safeguarding Adults in Social Work* 2nd edn (London: Sage)

Manthorpe, J, J Rapaport and N Stanley (2008) 'The Mental Capacity Act 2005 and its influences on social work practice: debate and synthesis' 20(3) *Practice* 151–62

McDonald, A (2007) 'The impact of the UK Human Rights Act 1998 on decision making in adult social care in England and Wales' 1(1) *Ethics and Social Welfare* 76–94

McDonald, A (2010) 'The impact of the 2005 Mental Capacity Act on social workers' decision making and approaches to the assessment of risk' 40 *British Journal of Social Work* 1229–46

McGhee, J and S Hunter (2011) 'The Scottish children's hearings tribunals system: a better forum for parents with learning disabilities?' 33(3) *Journal of Social Welfare and Family Law* 255–66

Ministry of Justice (2008) *Deprivation of Liberty Safeguards Code of Practice* (Norwich: The Stationery Office)

Rapaport, J, J Manthorpe and N Stanley (2009) 'Mental health and mental capacity law: some mutual concerns for social work' 21(2) *Practice* 91–105

Redley, M et al. (2011) 'Introducing the Mental Capacity Advocate (IMCA) Service and the Reform of Adult Safeguarding Procedures' 41 *British Journal of Social Work* 1058–69

Seymour, C and R Seymour (2013) *Practical Child Law for Social Workers* (London: Sage)

Social Care Institute for Excellence (2005) *Helping Parents with Learning disabilities in their Role as Parents* Research Briefing 14 (London: SCIE)

Social Care Institute for Excellence (2011) *Mental Capacity Act (MCA) Resource* (London: SCIE) www.scie.org.uk/publications/mca/index.asp

Social Care Institute for Excellence (2013) *Get Connected* www.scie.org.uk/ workforce/getconnected/index.asp

Tarleton, B and S Porter (2012) 'Crossing no man's land: a specialist support service for parents with learning disabilities' 17 *Child and Family Social Work* 233–43

Taylor, B (2010) *Professional Decision Making in Social Work Practice* (London: Sage)

Welsh Assembly Government (2000) *In Safe Hands* (Cardiff: Welsh Assembly Government)

Williams, V et al. (2012) *Making Best Interest Decisions: People and Processes* (London: Mental Health Foundation) www.mentalhealth.org.uk

INDEX